AN UNLIKELY AMBASSADOR AND HER DIPLOMATIC DAUGHTER

Mary Kramer

AN UNLIKELY AMBASSADOR AND HER DIPLOMATIC DAUGHTER

Stories and Recipes for the Life You Want

Amb Mary E Kramer (RET.)
and
Krista Kramer Hartman

an Optimistic Mother-Daughter Duo

ISBN: 1512142131
ISBN 13: 9781512142136
Library of Congress Control Number: 2015907675
CreateSpace Independent Publishing Platform
North Charleston, South Carolina

Dedications

To Kay

"My best friend and most supportive life partner."

From Mary

To Scott

"My champion, rock and chief dream adopter. You're the best!"

From Krista

To all those who came before us and helped shape our lives

"Together we dedicate this book to you.
We are eternally grateful."

From Mary and Krista

Acknowledgements

With our biggest thanks to:

Catherine Knepper - *our fabulous editor who has mastered Gem Number Three; Listen, Gem Number 4, Praise; Gem Number Six, Be Patient, But Not Toooo; Gem Number Eight, Endlessly Pleasant, Gem Number Ten, Lighten Up, and Gem Number Fifteen, Continuous Improvement. Thank you Catherine!*

Our Family Members *who you will meet as you read our book - just being part of our family deserves our appreciation.*

Our Friends *who have offered continual support, suggestions and advice through this long process.*

Nexus members *who early on offered suggestions, listened graciously as the book morphed into several "editions" and were ever supportive to both Krista and Mary.*

Special Note to Workshop Planners and Book Club Readers

*Mary and Krista regularly offer workshops designed to help individuals
and now our readers develop their personal vision of the desired future,
build teams,
and or polish their personal leadership skill set.*

Mary can be contacted at kaynmary@gmail.com
Krista can be contacted at kkhartman@gmail.com

Table of Contents

Our Big Idea

The impetus behind this book—the Big Idea that compels us to share—is a well-known bit of wisdom whose truth has been borne out in our lives and through the ages:

"To whom much is given, much is expected."

Mary & Krista Hawkeye Football Game 1995

We are a mother/daughter team and we have been given much! Between us we have decades of unusually diverse life experiences, complete with lots of change and lots of learning. It's the lessons we've learned on our inimitable journeys that compel us to share.

Mary, the mother in our story, grew up in Iowa and has been a piano player, a music teacher, a public school administrator, an author, a department store personnel officer, an insurance executive, a state senator, the state senate President, and a U.S. Ambassador. Krista, the daughter of our team, has been a semi-professional golfer, community leader, small business owner, and a serial entrepreneur. Together we've traveled the world, caused positive change in our communities, created a close-knit family, become leaders of our own lives, and dreamed dreams that we pursued and made happen. We're delighted to share our stories with you and tell you the specific steps we took in making *our* dreams come true in order to show you a way to make *your* dreams come true.

THE LEGACY OF GEMS

We have a Kramer family jewelry tradition. Kay, husband of 57 years to Mary and father of Krista, is generous in all respects, and perhaps especially so with gifts of jewelry. Over the years Mary has received many beautiful gems from Kay. Some are family heirlooms, but most are new pieces that Kay has selected. Each new gem is bigger and more beautiful than the last. And when that newer, shinier gem comes along, Krista, or Mary's daughter-in-law Kimberly, receives the previous one. Eventually those gems will be passed on to the next generation. The longer the gem has been in the family, the more valuable and meaningful it becomes. So you can see how "the legacy of gems" has become a cherished Kramer family tradition.

But of course, it's not just the literal gems that have been passed down…and it's the intangible gems that each generation bequeaths to the next that are far more precious. A value system. A strong work ethic. A love of family. Gratitude. The desire to dream big and then work to make those dreams happen. So in this book we will pass along the fifteen rhetorical gems that have served and continue to serve us so well. The more we wear (practice) and experience (apply) these rhetorical gems, the more effective, valuable and meaningful they become.

We hope you can use the Kramer Family Gems as an inspiration, a template to create your own legacy, for your individual life as well as within your own family.

Gem Number One: Cherish Family and Friends

It is important to "love and respect the elders" while celebrating the ideas and vision of new generations who add to the existing traditions while creating traditions of their own.

Kramers Celebrate Thanksgiving in Orlando 2014

MARY SAYS:

My childhood summers did not include camps or other organized activities. Opportunities weren't plentiful and we couldn't afford them anyway. There was no television in our home until I was in college. We played games and listened to favorite radio series in the evening. I never remember being bored. To this day, a wonderful option for me is staying home. Cooking or even doing chores offers its own pleasure, but having free time at home to daydream or to read is a luxury indeed.

Even though I was an only child, I was rarely lonely. During my early years, we lived next door to the Lotz family. Aunt Isabelle, Uncle Ed, cousins Mary Carolyn and Phillip. There was a shared driveway between our houses with two huge detached two-car garages in back. My Dad enjoyed raising goldfish, so there were several connected fishponds in our backyard. Perkins Park, just across the street, had crawdads, frogs, guppies and all manner of "wildlife" that were just fascinating. Every summer, the two garages were full of glass jars with lids poked full of holes that held interesting specimens and whatever we thought was food for them (usually leaves and grass). Our specimens usually had a shelf life of about 24 hours. We also had a cemetery in the corner of the back yard and almost every day we had a funeral or two for a goldfish or one of our specimens that didn't make it.

I loved reading and was allowed to take the city bus by myself to the Burlington Public Library on Saturday. I spent hours there, bringing home bags of books for the week's entertainment. Home was a great place for me. Playing with my cousins, helping Geneva in the kitchen, reading, playing the piano, visiting the farm and the library...all were stimulating pursuits that interested me.

Both Kay and I enjoyed our family dinner tables as we were growing up. After we were married, we decided that no matter how busy our schedules were there would be dinner together every night. We didn't care what time it was served and it was nothing fancy.

Not even well balanced by today's standards...tater tot casserole, mac and cheese, oven-barbequed chicken, meat that was fried, and potatoes that were mashed with butter—and always with dessert. We joke about a family favorite: "exotic" Jell-O. It consisted of any flavor of red Jell-O and a can of fruit cocktail. Whatever—we are all healthy! The important thing was the opportunity for conversation. To share the happenings of the day and to find out what was needed for tomorrow.

As a result of those family dinner tables, the idea of hospitality is firmly entrenched in my way of life. During the years I was in the retail business, it was understood that no one would be leaving town for Thanksgiving because all hands were on deck all weekend. Many of the merchants were young, single, and away from home so we included them at our Thanksgiving dinner table. Between family and friends, neighbors and my colleagues, we often had large and memorable gatherings.

When Kent was in fourth grade, we decided it would be a good idea to invite his teachers for lunch at our home. He was enthusiastic about the prospect. We needed to pick a date. The next day he issued the invitation for lunch—on that very day. I was dressed in jeans, sweatshirt and tennis shoes when I looked out the kitchen window and saw Kent and four of his teachers walking down the street toward our house! Peanut butter and jelly sandwiches were not going to be enough! Fortunately I had lettuce and vegetables to chop. I quickly hard boiled several eggs and opened a can of shrimp. We enjoyed shrimp salads with bread and butter and chocolate sundaes for dessert. Kent didn't realize he had done anything extraordinary—but his teachers knew how unprepared I was. We had a great time, and it is a sweet memory. I was thrilled that he was proud of his home and wanted to share it with his teachers. That was far more important than what was served for lunch.

Neither Kent nor Krista seemed to think it was anything out of the ordinary that both their father and mother worked outside the home, even though at the time it was unusual among their friends. Instead, they both seemed to believe that since someone would employ us, we were less likely to embarrass them in public. After all, someone thought we were smart enough to give us a job. As a result, our kids volunteered us to be the Cub Scout den mother, the Pinewood Derby supervisor, the homeroom parents, and the chairs of various booster clubs. The jobs needed to be done and our kids wanted us to do it. In spite of travel and work schedules, at least one of us attended all the musical performances and sporting events. It was a treat to see our kids doing so well. We were (still are) proud. We have had the privilege of enjoying many of those experiences with our granddaughters as well. I must admit however it is good to know there are no longer events that require us to sit on bleachers or chaperone field trips on school buses.

During our time in Barbados, many Americans on our staff could not afford to fly home or to take leave for holidays. Our Marines were never allowed to leave post. We were provided a lovely residence with a huge dining room table that could easily accommodate large groups. Chef Glen would inquire, "How many Marines, Madame Ambassador?" Usually the number was seven or eight, and off he'd go to add another turkey and another ham. People clearly enjoyed dining with us and they added so much to our lives. Happily, family and friends loved to visit us in Barbados for Thanksgiving and Christmas as well. We brought sweet corn seed back from our first trip back to Iowa. The Pyles at the Brighton Farmers Market raised and sold produce at their own farmers' market and agreed to try to grow it for us. It was a great success and we had Barbados-grown Iowa sweet corn on the cob for Christmas dinner, and it was delicious.

Thanksgiving in Barbados 2004

During the last year of my service as Ambassador, I found myself in near-constant pain. Walking and standing caused terrible pain in my hip. I knew I had a hip problem when I moved to the Caribbean, but I thought it was "a little arthritis," and that I could live with that.

I did live with it, but by the end of my service it was getting the better of me. During that last year I had weekly massages and acupuncture treatments to get temporary relief so I could keep going. After returning home I found a hip surgeon in Iowa and made an appointment. He showed me my x-ray and said, "Mary, your hip joint resembles the prickly club Fred Flintstone carried around in that TV cartoon years ago. That has to hurt. I can give you medication, but your only real choice is hip replacement surgery."

My only question? How soon can you do it?

The appointment was in early December, and the surgeon said most people didn't want the surgery just before the holidays so he could do it in a week if I wanted. I did! We got it done—and with an excellent surgeon we had excellent results and a great outcome. I was home 24 hours after surgery, walking with one crutch.

Christmas found everyone at home as usual that year. I learned I could delegate everything! (What a valuable learning experience that was!) Kay did the shopping, Krista and Kim did the cooking, everyone pitched in with cleanup. The family spent the time together and we had a great holiday.

My recovery was speedy and successful because of the support of my cherished family and our beloved family traditions. We still look forward to sharing holidays and gatherings with family today. The location and celebrating "on the exact day" are not important. Kent and Kim and Krista and Scott are generous and gracious hosts and there is always room for family, friends and colleagues at their dining room tables.

There's a postscript to the story of my hip. Five years later, my other hip felt left out and needed to be replaced. So back we went to the same surgeon—and with the support of my doctors and family I got the same results. I am walking with no restrictions, playing golf again (still badly) and enjoying a pain-free existence. My only problem, it seems, is traveling by air. I set off the alarms and have to be "wanded" every time I travel. Despite my "senior sage" appearance and Endlessly Pleasant persona, people take me for a dangerous person.

KRISTA SAYS:

The first important tradition I want to share is a "partnership in marriage" tradition where both spouses are professionals and honor their mutual desires to grow and advance in their careers. Mom and Dad conducted their relationship in exactly this way, and they were trailblazers. I am unaware of another couple of their generation who from the beginning set as one of the pillars of their marriage the idea of partnership or taking turns with professional opportunities. When Mom and Dad were newly married, both of their mothers were concerned that Mom working outside of the home would cause people to think Dad wasn't able to support her! Fortunately neither Mom nor Dad shared this concern, and Mom was free to pursue her ambitions. The Kramer "partnership in marriage" pillar is a 57+ year tradition that I've witnessed firsthand for nearly 50 years.

Kramers Celebrate Mary & Kay's 50th Anniversary Alaska Cruise June 13, 2008

Let me describe this tradition from the perspective of the "daughter of"—what I observed and experienced firsthand as the child of a couple who honored each other's professional aspirations. In the Mastery Gem you'll read later, Mom eloquently describes how the opportunity for Dad to make a big difference in the lives of schoolchildren with disabilities and their families was a tremendous opportunity. She also describes how that very career move required them to move from Iowa City to Des Moines just as she'd begun to bump against the glass ceiling in her own career, and how she had no desire to leave Iowa City. But they leaned on their established partnership in marriage tradition, developed over many previous moves and several career decisions, and weighed the decision according to their agreed-upon criteria: Would it be most beneficial to the family, and would it make a difference? The answer to both questions was yes, so Mom resigned from her position, Dad accepted the new offer, and off they went to Des Moines.

It was the right move for all concerned. Dad did make a big difference in childhood education for children with disabilities, and Mom ended up with bigger and better career opportunities than she could have anticipated.

This is just one example among many of how they really did take turns. One Master's degree at a time while the other one worked and earned, one career move forward for one, while the other stayed put in the current position and was the supporter and quarterback at home with Kent and me. I know career opportunities and moves fit into the mixture many times for both Mom and Dad, and they only enhanced our family life, and did not force either partner to make a potentially undesirable change in their career. It may not have been easy each time there was a turn to be taken, or a change made, but living up to their commitment to this tradition says so much about the strength of their marriage and partnership together for all these 57+ years.

I believe this belongs in our discussion of tradition because it sets such a great example. I sought out a spouse and partner who would respect and embrace this tradition and be willing to adopt it as a custom in our marriage partnership, too. This gives true meaning to the tenet of equality in marriage—and the kind of equality that doesn't privilege one gender over another. Mary and Kay's example, their approach and commitment to marriage as a partnership, exemplifies what it means to respect our partner's ability to succeed as an independent professional while maintaining a healthy, solid, loving marriage.

Scott and I have encountered the opportunity to put this tradition to use twice in our life together thus far. The first time occurred when I was starting to feel "up against the wall" in a job where I'd become miserable and felt unwanted. Leaving and diving into residential real estate meant forfeiting my salary and benefits, and switching to a 100% commission-based earning style. We weren't yet married, but Scott assured me he was sticking with me and that making this change was going to turn out as the right direction for me to go. It was tough, but having faith in the idea that he was giving me a "turn" to try out a risky, yet desirable job while he supported me and our shared home financially and as my cheerleader was amazing.

Four years after this transition, we'd been married for about three years and an opportunity for him to traverse the career ladder in corporate America came along. And it meant we were moving to Dallas. It meant that my four years of building a residential real estate business would be concluding because it was his turn, and it was a tremendous opportunity for him at that time in his career. I leaned on the memories of Mom and Dad's career changes and was able to talk with both Mom and Dad during this time. As a result I felt content and secure in the choices Scott and I were making together, as partners.

Finally, no commentary about our family traditions would be complete without sharing about IOWA! Our family has a deep loyalty to the great state of Iowa and to the University of Iowa. Our DNA is ALL IOWA. As I have sorted through a lifetime of photos while writing our book, I have stumbled upon memories of our Iowa families that cover four generations. Memories of their homes—with their cherished heirlooms like desks, special chairs, steamer trunks, and Spode Pink Tower dishes—are so vivid, as are the different communities we'd take a drive to for church and Sunday dinner, or a wedding or a reunion near Burlington or Forest City. I also remember driving to Remsen to visit my Kramer grandparents; when we saw the church steeple for the Catholic church over the hilly horizon we'd know we were getting close. I can also visualize that road with a crazy amount of snowfall as we drove there one Thanksgiving. I remember my Great Uncle Clyde delivering fresh sweet corn from the family farms directly to my Barnett grandparents' home on Brookland Park Drive in Iowa City. As I entered my twenties I have to add memories of funerals and a cold snowy cemetery in Remsen.

But there are also happy memories from great, sunny places where we'd spend time with friends in the summer, like Lake Okoboji. There's nothing that triggers tons of great memories such as the thought of Iowa City on a cool autumn sunny morning when the town is buzzing for an afternoon Iowa football game.

Krista & Herky the Hawk 1999

In *IOWA: A Celebration of Land, People & Purpose*, a book that commemorates Iowa's sesquicentennial, Iowa native and internationally renowned journalist Hugh Sidey wrote, "Iowa is that special place which has crafted itself to claim a big part of the future, but never sacrificed those values of person and community on which a successful society must rest. From my perch, I see Iowa as a unique blend of land and people and purpose." Growing up in Iowa equipped me to appreciate land, people and purpose, just as Sidey stated. I often refer to Iowa as "my version of God's Country." There's a song titled "In God's Country" by U2, and I wonder if Bono would understand that when I listen to it, I can't help but crave a taste of my Iowa memories. I can listen and enjoy this song and in my imagination replay my internal Technicolor videotapes of so many Iowa landscapes and family memories.

Occasionally we would adventure outside the borders of Iowa into—wait for it—Minnesota and Missouri, Kansas, even Illinois. These were fun trips to explore the metropolises of elsewhere and to have fun meeting up with grandparents, aunts, uncles and cousins;

usually a professional sports event like pre-season football or a base-ball game was involved, as was back-to-school shopping.

As I have matured and grown up, I've been able to carry on many of my family traditions. A lot of them involve cooking and eating together due to the immense library of recipes our combined families have accumulated. I thoroughly enjoy preparing a brunch or a meal for special occasions for groups of family or friends. Here I use recipes from Mom & Dad, Dick & MaryAnn Rosonke, Aunt Carol, Aunt Nancy and so many others. Outside of a handful of top secret "for Kramer eyes only" recipes, Mom has created a family cookbook bringing together the "best of" all Kramer, Barnett, and travel recipes from a long history of years in the kitchen. As our way of passing along some of our cooking traditions with you, you'll find several meaningful family recipes to enjoy in the final pages of this book.

Thanksgiving has long been one of my favorite meals not only to prepare and cook for, but also in creating a guest list. When Mom worked for Younkers, she and Dad started hosting the "retail orphans," staff who were scheduled to work the Friday, Saturday and Sunday following Thanksgiving and couldn't travel to be with their families. This turned into a tradition of hosting the "orphans" no matter where either Mom or Dad worked, or where they lived.

When they were in Barbados in the early 2000's, they'd in-clude the Marines in the Ambassador's residence for Thanksgiving, Christmas and Easter dinners, to let them know they were consid-ered family. As Scott and I now live 1,000+ miles away from our families, on many holidays we've found ourselves to be the new generation of orphans! We've happily continued Mom and Dad's tradition of hosting orphans, and have made it a priority to provide a family-style meal, warm environment, and meaningful fellowship for our "orphaned" friends who are also far from family for special holidays like Thanksgiving and Easter. There's something really heartening about preparing a special, usually traditional menu (with a twist) for the gathering on a holiday with people who are dear to us. Our guests give us rave reviews.

Another Kramer family tradition is hand-me-downs. Is this practice still alive and well today? Our society is too quick to throw away items of perfectly good quality, and to lean too heavily on disposable items. But we grew up with plenty of fabulous hand-me-downs. I had two older girl cousins, and clothing (often handmade), dolls (with handmade clothes to match), toys, musical instruments and much more were handed down to me. In our family, Dale Norwegian sweaters were handed down and have now made it at least two generations.

Krista, Kelsey & Kallen Norwegian Sweaters 1996

Golf clubs have been another "handed down" item, too. First from Dad to Kent, Mary to Kris—then Kent to Kris, then Dad to Kent or Kris again, from Kris to Idalia "DiDi" (our favorite caddy at Sandy Lane in Barbados) and from Kris to a few friends. It's like dominoes sometimes—when one person matures or splurges on a new set of irons or woods, at least one or two other people in our family or circle of friends have benefitted. In fact, it wasn't until the summer of 2014 that Kent purchased a new set of clubs for himself. (I think he claims it was during high school when he purchased his own Walter Hagen irons with money he earned working part-time at Younkers or from de-tasseling corn.)

It's no secret my Dad likes golf and golf equipment and gadgets. And for many years when he travelled frequently, he'd have two of everything, one for a home bag and one for a travel bag. This is where you can be assured that Kent and I, and Scott, too, have been spoiled and blessed with great golf gear thanks to Dad and his handing stuff down. (Which by the way, is another excellent way to "pay it forward," our Gem Number Five.) I was excited last summer to be able to share some golf shirts and hats with my niece Kennedy who has some interest in golf. YES!

Krista & Kennedy Golfing at Hyperion 2013

For me, a tradition doesn't have to be kept each and every year on the occasion of every year. It's become more meaningful for the tradition to be kept when all the parties involved in the origination of the tradition can be assembled to make it happen and ensure it's real to each person involved. For niece Kallen and Eric's wedding, I built their gift around a French dish, Coq Au Vin, which I have claimed as one of my traditional menu items (see Big Plates). And for niece Kelsey and her groom KC, I built their gifts around cookie baking, which has been a long-standing family tradition we've all enjoyed together for years (see Desserts).

For my final thought around the ideas of tradition, I'd like you to remember the phrase, "Don't ask, just pour." This is a famous phrase my Grandpa Kramer coined in the mid 80's while several of us were gathered in Minneapolis for a summer visit. During what could be termed family happy hour, we were all in Mom and Dad's hotel room talking, having some cheeses and crackers, and a glass of wine. I asked Grandpa if he'd like some wine and he replied, "Don't ask, just pour." So from that moment on until the last time I visited my grandfather, I did not ask, I just poured. I now do the same at any gathering. The implied message from Grandpa Cyril that will stick with me forever is if I'm going to pour and enjoy for myself (and I know I will) I will also pour for others and let them enjoy and savor as well. It warms my heart to remember that moment with Cyril George Kramer, one of my two progressive Iowa granddads!

For You to Say:

- Describe your most cherished traditions. Are you nurturing those in your relationships and in your family?
- What traditions would you like to add to your experiences? How will you go about creating them?
- What holidays do you celebrate? What are the foods, places and people that make them memorable?
- Do you keep a journal of these traditions? If not, consider doing so! You'll be giving a precious gift to every successive generation.

Gem Number Two: A Vision of the Desired Future is Necessary!

"Without vision, people perish." Proverbs 29:18

MARY SAYS:

Maybe you're already asking, *"Great...whose vision and how do I get it?"*

Answer? Create it.

Here's how I do it. It's not rocket science. The future you envision for yourself will include your job, your family, your volunteer roles—any or all of the above. Try to include the whole picture. Why is vision so crucial? Because when we are able to clearly communicate a vision of the desired future, we can enlist followers in noble causes with meaning and purpose. That vision becomes a *shared* vision of the desired future. Noble causes are not limited to a job or financial success. They include staying healthy, raising children who become contributors to society, leading team(s) to accomplish big agendas, or encouraging volunteers to do the work that makes a difference in the neighborhood, in the church, and in the community.

Being intentional about your own desired future and writing it down is empowering and one of the most powerful learnings of my life. If you don't know where you're going, any road will take you there and few will want to go with you.

Creating a vision requires a blank sheet of paper, a pen or pencil, some time to think, and the courage to write. Decide how far into the future you want to look. It might be a day, a week, a month, a year. For me the year is the most effective. Any longer than a year gets a bit foggy, and shorter time periods lead me to short-term thinking. I review my vision every year sometime in my birthday month.

So get pencil and paper and answer these questions:

- WHERE AM I NOW? (Stuck? In a good place? Ready to make a leap? In need of a new skill?)
- WHERE DO I WANT TO BE ONE YEAR (you pick the time frame) FROM NOW?
- WHO WILL BE WITH ME? (Spouse, friends, children, colleagues, co-workers, etc.)
- HOW WILL I GET THERE? (What actions do I need to complete?)
- WHAT WILL BE IMPORTANT AND HOW WILL I KNOW? (What will change, and how do I measure that change?
- WHAT RESOURCES WILL BE REQUIRED AND HOW CAN I GET THEM? (Money, time, health changes, relationship changes, etc.)

I completed that first vision many years ago and now I follow my process annually, usually in my birthday month.

First, I review what I wrote the previous year. Some things can be **crossed off** the list. They're complete, I have lost interest, or maybe I've experienced a wake-up call about that particular goal. (Sometimes I read what I wrote the previous year and think to myself, "Perhaps you were enjoying a little too much wine when you wrote this, Mary?")

I **highlight** the items that are incomplete or that I need to continue doing.

I **make a list** of the new ideas that I want to consider this year.

Finally, I **spend a little time celebrating** accomplishments—just for myself.

Truthfully, there have been years in which I just looked at the page and thought, *I could just put a new date on this one.*

This process was a little scary at first. Many people I have worked with to create a personal vision/mission statement resist writing anything down. Their fear? When something is written on the page it becomes tangible and they believe they must accomplish that goal no matter what. They're afraid that if they don't achieve every single thing they have written, they have failed.

NOT SO!

Remember, *you are in control* of your list and your decisions. Sometimes I check my list during the year and realize I didn't want to do that thing after all. In that case I just cross it off the list. No harm done! Later in the book you will read: Mastery is optional.

On the other hand, sometimes I check the list because I know I have accomplished something—and it just feels good to check it off as an accomplishment.

And that's it. Don't over-think it or try to make it perfect. Neatness and spelling do not count. If it makes you feel better, use a pencil—after all very few people do the crossword puzzles in ink! Keep it simple...complete sentences are not necessary. This is just a method of organizing your thinking. It doesn't need to be shared with anyone, unless you find it helpful. *Please try it.* It's impossible to plan for a desired future, to be specific about what you are seeking, or to talk about your vision for that desired future unless *you know* what that desired future looks like.

When I was in the insurance business, the company needed a new CEO. The man conducting the search asked me to develop my résumé and apply for the position. I was flattered, and began to consider the possibilities of being the Chief Executive Officer. The Company had a series of problems that I understood very well. It was and would continue to be a volatile time in the health insurance industry. I spent time and money developing my résumé, and I got some coaching about how to interview for this position. I had included in my vision statement a promotion with additional responsibility, but I had not considered the idea of the CEO. So the interviews began, I had a look at other candidates, and I actually made it to the final round.

But some of the questions in that final interview led me to believe I was included because they needed a woman candidate and an insider candidate. They could check off both those boxes with me. To this day I'm not sure whether I was ever seriously considered. Why share this? Because in my visioneering I knew I needed a change and had in my vision statement my desire for additional or different responsibilities. I learned a lot from the interview process. All my options for advancement were not within the company, my résumé included a broad variety of successful leadership positions, and I understood a lot more about myself after working on an updated résumé and being coached to think about my answers to possible interview experiences. All good things—more change was coming!

This experience also helped me realize I had been limiting my dreams and goals to what I thought I could achieve. No really big dreams. No really risky goals. I needed to expand my vision. There is a lot of opportunity out there, and as a result of this process I saw a way forward to go find some of that opportunity.

KRISTA SAYS:

Mom's vision statement is one of my favorite exercises. I've shared these simple questions in speeches and I've customized them into Power Point presentations and into mini notebooks for clients (and friends) who feel stuck. These are simple ideas in question form that you can use at any time you choose.

These questions **may be the catalyst you need** to make a change or start a new habit, or bring about a small shift in your thinking to help you take the next step... or nudge you a little bit. I do believe taking the time to answer these questions will make you feel more focused and self-directed. Focus and direction are part of feeling and of *being* successful.

Give yourself permission to step out of your way for a few minutes, get your view in focus and commit to creating a vision for yourself and your desired future. This is what I call **Visioneering.**

Mom likes to do this on her birthday, in June, on the deck on a beautiful summer afternoon—with wine. I usually work on my Visioneering statement between Thanksgiving and Christmas (also with wine), and at the same time I begin to wrap up my business year. (It helps me avoid tax preparation procrastination, too.)

I love to include with the instructions for Visioneering: **Get specific, intentional, purposeful and strategic.** This helps you to be innovative, collaborative and ready to accelerate. Give yourself credit where and when you deserve it. Be real with YOURSELF as you answer these simple questions.

And remember—*it's meant to be revised. Visioneering is change-capable, just like our real, God-given eyesight.*

For You To Say:

- How can you become more intentional? Do you think developing a written vision would help?
- Can you think of an example when a written vision would help you to make an important decision?
- Are there barriers preventing you from developing a personal vision? What are they? How can you work to stretch beyond them?
- How do you or how will you recognize and celebrate your accomplishments?

Gem Number Three: Listen

Knowledge talks. Wisdom listens.

MARY SAYS:

I often begin leadership development classes by asking participants a multiple-choice question, answered by a show of hands:
What do you expect to take away from the class today?

a.) Get my ideas across more forcefully
b.) Write a better memo
c.) Tell a great joke
d.) Become a better listener

There is always a mix of answers, but few people select d) become a better listener. Why? Because listening is believed to be something that just happens, not something that requires our attention and effort. People tend to think that listening isn't an active pursuit, or something that requires skill and practice. Worse, rarely is listening considered a skill associated with leadership, when in reality, excellent listening skills are one of the paramount requirements of being an excellent leader.

Great listeners maintain eye contact, listen to every word without interrupting or offering advice, and ask only clarifying questions. Great listeners acknowledge what they heard by paraphrasing what the speaker said, without judgment and without correcting.

Try this exercise: How many ways can you interpret this sentence? Put emphasis on a different word each time you repeat it aloud. **I did not say he stole the money.** There are six possible interpretations of this one sentence! Only after listening and clarifying the meaning can we understand what others are hearing...and only then can we move forward to define problems, to find common ground, to consider solutions.

Now try this exercise. List three or four people you consider to be your best friends. Now prioritize them according to who listens best. Is it surprising to realize that the friends and family you consider the best listeners are the same people that you respect and trust the most? Listening demonstrates respect. It is the highest of compliments because it clearly shows that the listener values the thoughts and ideas of the speaker. True listening invariably enhances relationships. When you show respect, trust, and love, those feelings are returned to you many times over.

Ambassador Mary E. Kramer with Secretary of
State James A. Baker III circa 2010

Children (and adults too for that matter) often become frustrated when things don't go their way immediately. The first reaction is to place blame (adults are guilty of this, too). As a teacher, I learned that simply raising my voice and putting a stop to an argument did not lead to resolution. A more successful method involves asking questions.

In the Iowa Legislature the arguments about whether to allow parents to homeschool their children had been ongoing for years. Each side of the argument just kept repeating their position, escalating the volume and expanding the rhetoric. As a newcomer to the Senate, I was appointed to a conference committee with two of the strongest proponents of their respective positions. Because of many constituent calls, most senators wanted to at least *appear* to be searching for a solution. At the first meeting, the two men sat down, pushed their chairs back from the table and folded their arms over their chests. Their body language sent a very clear message: *I'm not playing!* I asked if anyone could identify an area of agreement, any common ground that would allow us to begin a real discussion. But they only restated their positions—they could not even *listen* to the other's position. So I said, "Then let's just disband the committee and announce that we cannot reach an agreement. I see no point in continuing to repeat the same arguments."

Whoa! Suddenly other committee members had ideas and suggestions. Apparently they wanted to play after all! After listening carefully to both sides, I said, "These are great ideas. This impasse has been going on for many years. My constituents want us to deal with this. Can we help?"

Ideas like "there have to be standards" and "the school district could still receive the state allowance for each child if they allowed participation in extracurricular activities" and "the kids could take the same standardized tests as everyone else to be sure they were progressing" were put forth and had merit for everyone. The discussion moved away from the "my way or no way" to tangible suggestions that caused people to start listening to each other. We passed a bill that session. Neither man voted for it, but we found enough common ground to resolve the impasse and move the issue forward.

Though we've made great strides in this area, it is true that women are interrupted during discussion more often than men. So, it is helpful to have an appropriate tactic for making sure your ideas are heard. When I took my place at an executive management table the first time, I was the first and only women officer of the company, and I was interrupted often during meetings. After being cut off several times, I made the "time out" sign (fingers of one hand to the palm of the other hand) and asked, "Does everyone get a turn to talk?" The group agreed—a little sheepishly—and I was given a chance to speak.

It took a while for the management team to learn some good listening skills. Any time I was interrupted, I would again make the time-out sign, and then say (with some humor), "I thought it was MY turn to talk." Then I could complete my thoughts. After a couple of those efforts, the "time out" sign was enough: I was given the floor and was able to complete my thought uninterrupted. And eventually, I didn't need to use the signal at all.

KRISTA SAYS:

Because music has always been an important component in our family life, I think we Kramers learned to appreciate listening skills in a different way. The skill and gem about listening has developed in my world over time through keen observation. I watch how others listen (and respond) during a performance, at meetings, at family gatherings, during discussions, and in church or worship settings. Through this habit of processing what I'm hearing while listening in any of the above situations I ask myself, "What do I do with what I am hearing? What meaning does it create for me?" Then I can choose the most effective way to participate.

In learning the piano, you "listen" to hear two hands and how they work together (or not), and once you add a pedal with your feet, there's more to listen for. In learning the violin and guitar, you "listen" and know immediately whether or not your finger is specifically on the right fret to create the "in tune" note or chord. In learning to play in a group—concert band, jazz band, chamber ensemble, or just jamming in the garage—you hear various melodies coming together to create a beautiful harmonic combination. If you are listening carefully, you can point to what is being produced and judge—is this what the composer intended? When singing the harmony as part of a group, there's something incredibly rewarding and energizing when the sounds you are producing confirm you are singing in tune, and that you're creating something far greater than the sum of its parts.

This carries over to conversational style. Listening to another person takes practice as well. It takes practice to not interject and interrupt—to permit your conversation partner to complete his or her thought before responding. It takes practice to truly tune into the words being conveyed by the other person rather than immediately crafting a response in your mind. It takes practice to allow for a short period of silence in between the conclusion of one person's thoughts and the introduction of the other person's response. It also takes practice not to immediately begin offering advice.

On my first day of art class in seventh grade, our teacher made the guidelines for commenting on another person's work of art very clear: "If you can't say something nice, don't say anything." There was zero tolerance for mean criticism of another person's creative efforts and what their imagination produced. This was a good lesson that has stuck with me. It was much easier to listen to the discussion of our art projects when we knew there would not be "mean" comments.

Listening for me is part of the "reading people" skill. Too often, due to one participant's tendencies to make incorrect assumptions, draw quick conclusions, and settle on unfortunate interpretations, even the expectation that your conversation partner is in fact listening is lost. Being constantly "plugged in" to technology makes listening even more difficult. It is impossible to listen while emailing, texting or instant messaging. Today, the lack of person-to-person, face-to-face interactions makes the human art and skill of listening ever more valuable. Listening well means listening to every word without interrupting—of giving your conversation partner the gift of your silence, so he or she can give you the gift of his or her words. When the speaker finishes, acknowledge what you heard without judging or correcting. Then ask for clarification if you need to: Did I hear you correctly?

One of my favorite quotes is: "If you don't understand my silence how will you understand my words?" Listening well is truly an art, and it is one of the highest forms of respect we can offer to the people around us.

For You to Say:

- If you're not accustomed to thinking of listening as an active skill, try it out for a few days. Bring intention and active focus to the times you listen to others, and note the difference in your conversations.
- How would you rate your listening skills today?
- What are some techniques you could use to become a more "active" listener?
- Who could help you improve your listening skills?
- What is your comfort level with silence?
- Practice increasing your comfort zone for silence in order to allow others to formulate and express their thoughts.

Gem Number Four: Praise

Praise and recognition, sincerely given,
are the most powerful tools in your toolbox.

MARY SAYS:

For her grandchildren's birthdays, Grandma McElhinney always baked an angel food cake, handmade "from scratch," especially for that child. What made it so remarkable was her patience. There was no electric mixer to produce the light, fluffy egg whites required for angel food cake: She beat the egg whites by hand with a wire whisk until they were exactly the right consistency—no quick, easy process! The birthday boy or girl got to sit at her knee and sift in the dry Ingredients using the old-fashioned crank sifter. (All the grown-ups got cakes too, but they did not get to help sift or frost.) It seemed to take a very long time, but sitting with her and turning the crank of the sifter felt like an immense, important job. She praised the effort continually. The frosting required egg white, sugar and vanilla. The end product was a *huge* cake covered with white frosting that had swirls like the ocean and pink candles for the girls and blue candles for the boys. She praised that cake as though the child had done it all by herself. It sat on the beautiful cut glass pedestal cake plate for all to see and admire. Standing behind that cake to blow out the candles with all the aunts, uncles and cousins watching was a special moment. I do not remember any of the gifts I received on those early birthdays, but I will always remember the sifting, the frosting, and the candles. It was my day with Grandma and a celebration of my day. Those birthday celebrations made it clear every grandchild was appreciated and loved. Recognition, celebration and love that honors birthdays and other milestones and victories cannot be overdone.

Mary's Third Birthday Cake 1938

During my first year of teaching, I was the director of an eighth grade mixed chorus. It began as a pitiful group, with only a few girls and even fewer boys. It was clearly not a "cool" activity. One of the boys was thought to be "academically challenged" and so was sent to mixed chorus to fill his schedule. He happened to be the son of one of the two African-American families in the community. I quickly learned he had a wonderful singing voice, but he could not read the words. No wonder he was considered "academically challenged"—he could not read! He was a fine athlete as well as a fine singer and was in danger of being ineligible for competition at the high school level because of his grades—and his attitude. He needed help, and I knew he could be a magnet for raising the interest of other boys in the chorus. So I made him a proposition. I would teach him to read the words if he would help me recruit other boys to sing in the chorus. I had no idea how to teach reading, but I thought he could learn phonetically like I did—repeating the words to songs during rehearsal would help him to figure them out.

And that's just what happened. He figured out the magic of sounding words out, realized he was not stupid, and applied himself to learning to read. I asked him to sing a solo in the spring concert that first year, "Swing Low, Sweet Chariot," with the chorus backing him up. The kid brought down the house. He was a rock star immediately! The applause and recognition he received for his ability to perform so beautifully changed his life. I know it did because during his high school career he and his parents told me so—often. What a wonderful success for that young man—and for that first-year music teacher.

Presenting a beautiful meal or a special dessert (especially a homemade pie) has created occasions when I have received praise many times. As a newlywed, I decided I needed a dinner menu that I could do perfectly, so we could invite dinner guests and I was sure everything would be fine. I had a recipe file where I kept a record of who came to dinner and what I served to be sure I didn't serve the same thing to the same people. My go-to dinner menu included a poached chicken (from Julia Child) a rice dish, green peas with chervil and parsley, an apricot Jell-o salad (we did live in Iowa, after all), and a chocolate cream pie for dessert (from The Bell File). (In our recipe section in the final pages, you'll find the poached chicken recipe in the Big Plates section, and the chocolate cream pie filling in the Desserts Section). I still enjoy making and eating these dishes. And I still love to entertain guests for dinner or parties. We have a traditional holiday open house each year at Christmastime. The party gives me the excuse to make classy hors d'oeuvres and rich desserts I rarely make any other time of year. I love preparing the food and welcoming our guests, and I always receive lavish praise on our food and decor. It's a joyful, special time for everyone involved.

Here are a few simple methods of providing positive recognition:

- Address people by name.
- Say Thank You. In person, via email, sometimes a handwritten note or letter. People remember your thanking them forever.
- Instead of giving orders, respectfully ask for assistance.
- When providing a critique, always recognize something good before you offer suggestions for change. In the retail business, some store managers marched through their stores every morning like Sherman marching through Georgia: Fold this, move that, put those in front, straighten that. They leave a trail of anger and disappointment behind them. How much more effective to say, "That looks good, let's move these things here," and then pause to help.
- Give people praise and thanks from time to time. "Great job!" "I really appreciate how you did that." "Good work on that project." "I liked how you did [fill in the blank]." These simple forms of recognition and appreciation do not cost anything but do require practice so they become habit.

And don't forget to give *yourself* a positive message! *"You rock, Mary!"* followed by a fist pump works for me.

KRISTA SAYS:

In high school I was an elected member of the Student Senate, the leadership body of the school. Even so, I didn't see myself as a leader per se, certainly not in the sense of handing out orders. What I did know was that I was capable of visualizing and articulating my desired outcomes and expectations for the Senate's objectives. Because I could communicate those goals and do what it took to reach them, I had loyal followers who would adopt my dreams and ideas. My enthusiasm and gratitude for their help was like praise to them. The spirit of cooperation among a small group of us created fun and close camaraderie: We thoroughly enjoyed doing whatever we had organized ourselves to do. Here's a place I'm hoping I said thank you enough to all the friends involved: Patty, Terri, Joe, Ian, Jeff, and many others. And even if I did, I want to say it again, 30+ years later! You can't thank people enough who are serving with you and supporting you as a leader.

As an officer on the board of my sorority in college I served in the role of PACE– Personal And Chapter Enrichment leader. This meant I was the resource and voice for enthusiasm, staying positive and providing encouragement to my sisters for many aspects of their college experiences. The job happened to arrive at the time in my life when I was struggling academically because of severe test anxiety. But I did not let my struggles show in my role as PACE. It was my job to lift up my sorority sisters, and help them feel good about themselves in all aspects of their college life. So, I put on my "suck it up" suit and did what a lot of women have to do (no offense, guys).

Women are really good at caregiving, and at putting other people ahead of themselves. It makes us feel good, and we like to build others up. You can't help but feel better about yourself when you are making other people feel better about themselves.

My first opportunity as a professional manager came during my college internship. At age 22, I was directing a team of high school and college age staff in a golf pro shop. Because of my enthusiasm for the job, from everything to unpacking golf shirts to merchandising putters, drivers, and balls, I was able to make what could have been tedious tasks exciting. And because I was raised to ask nicely for things, say thank you, and extend verbal praise for a job well done, I don't recall having any trouble with leading or managing my team. Lessons I'd learned at home from my parents and my grandparents extended seamlessly to the work environment.

In a similar spirit of Mom's cake-making with her Grandma McElhinney, I fondly remember making cut-out cookies with her for holidays—Thanksgiving, Christmas, Valentine's Day, Easter, and more. It was such a fun production, getting out the recipe from the big file drawer, the ingredients, the sprinkles, colored sugars, the various cookie cutters and tools we would use just a few times each year together, and then making the dough, rolling it out, and cutting dozens of cookies. And just as Mom described, the appreciation and love that came along with a day in the kitchen together was fabulous.

I enjoyed making candies and cookies at my Barnett grandparents' house during the holidays as well. They made so many candies and cookies they seemed to have a mini confectionary factory every Christmas season—even the guest beds were covered with large trays of goodies waiting to be packaged for sharing. I felt very special and grownup when I was invited to help. The cookies and candies were placed in fancy metal canisters and Grandpa would mail or personally deliver these containers to 40-50 families. Mom liked to joke that after Grandpa retired, he thought he was Fannie May.

When I became an Auntie, I began my own tradition of making cut-out sugar cookies with my nieces during Christmas vacations. In the early years, they lived in Raleigh and I lived in Chicago, so it was the one of the few times I was able to spend quality time with them in Iowa. We would take over my mom's large kitchen counter top and make bells, stars, angels, trees, Santas, and candy canes. It was quite a process. We made the dough, rolled the dough, cut out the shapes, baked, and then came the best part—the creative frosting. I hoped and prayed that my nieces would cherish the special time with their Auntie Krista and remember the anticipation of the invitation to "play" in the kitchen together. They took great pride in their contributions to the three-tiered dessert display on the Kramer family Christmas Eve buffet, and I took care to praise their efforts and their unique artistic visions. Those cookie-baking sessions continue to be a multigenerational gem in themselves (see Anna's Rolled Sugar Cookies in Desserts).

Krista, Kelsey, & Kallen Baking Cut-Out Cookies 1996

For You to Say:

- Do you have special memories about times you were praised and your feelings towards those who offered that praise?
- How could you be more cognizant of recognizing praise opportunities?
- Who are the people in your life who would value your praise and recognition most?
- Who praises you now? Your spouse/significant other, your friends, your parents, other loved ones? Your boss?
- Set goals for saying please, thank you, and "good job," and pay attention to the reactions of those around you.

Gem Number Five: Give Back, Pay it Forward

Action steps for "To whom much is given, much is expected." Luke 12:48

MARY SAYS:

Kay has no patience for long meetings. When he agreed to serve on the Session of St. Andrew's Presbyterian Church in Iowa City it only took two meetings lasting from 7 PM until midnight for him to realize some process changes were necessary if he was to continue. He discussed options with our friend and attorney, also a member of the Session. They both realized that some members of the group enjoyed the social aspects of conversation much more than staying on point and sticking with an agenda. They viewed the meetings as their night out. Not the best way to get the church business accomplished!

So Kay and his attorney friend announced to their colleagues that they would be leaving each meeting at 10 PM—if there were critical agenda items that required them to vote, those things should be brought up before 10 PM. Shocker!

Kay and his colleague faced accusations about poor stewardship from some, but they got support from others. Several members thanked them profusely, saying this really needed to happen. And guess what? The meetings began to operate more efficiently, discussions stayed on point and the work got done, often *before* 10 PM.

Kay's contribution to the improved procedure was at least as important as the substance of the meeting. People stayed focused on the business at hand, which led to greatly improved decision-making. Now that the time commitment was clear, other people were willing to volunteer who hadn't been before. Because it is volunteer service does not mean there shouldn't be every effort to make things better. Giving back and paying it forward sometimes involves changing processes so that better outcomes are possible.

When I was in a leadership position at Younkers, a tragedy that occurred on my watch taught me some of the hardest lessons I ever learned about leadership—but it also demonstrated the healing and the support that can occur when a company is invested in giving it back and paying it forward to its employees.

On a Sunday morning shortly after Kay and I got home from church the phone rang. It was the manager of Younkers at the Merle Hay Mall. There was a bad fire at the store, and there could be employees trapped inside—could I come right away? Of course I could.

When I got there I knew immediately it was bad. The firefighters and emergency units were everywhere, and black smoke was still pouring out of the building. The brick walls were charred and black, and the glass was broken out of windows and doors. The fire chief and the chief of the emergency units introduced themselves and warned me that the damage was extensive. The media arrived shortly after I did and coverage began immediately. And shortly after that, family members began showing up, looking for loved ones who had been at work in the building.

The employees who had come in on a Sunday morning were working to be sure the payroll was finished on time. No one had asked them to be there—they were concerned about their fellow employees getting paid. It was just the sort of conscientious, "give it back and pay it forward" people they were.

Leaders of the company were en route to the market in New York, so the store manager and I were the "go-to" spokespersons and decision makers. I introduced myself to family members, told them I would keep them informed as I learned anything, and if they wanted to go home we would call. They all stayed nearby, most just waiting in their cars. Looking at the destroyed building, it was hard to have hope. But we all waited together, with equal parts fear and hope. The Red Cross and the Salvation Army arrived with coffee and sandwiches—for the firefighters, the emergency personnel, and those of us waiting for news. It was very cold—below freezing with a drizzling rain.

After several hours, the firefighters let us know that the fire was under control, they'd been able to enter the building and yes, there were fatalities.

About two hours after that, the Medical Examiner came to me with more specific information. The news was not good. Ten Younkers employees had died in that fire.

Nothing can prepare you for a disaster of this magnitude.

It was hard to control my own emotions—these were people I knew well. I had to deliver the news to family members, and provide whatever comfort and support I could. I had no knowledge or experience to understand the steps that must be taken in situations like this, but I did the best I could.

Later in the afternoon, I began to think about all the other Younkers employees who would be out of work, beginning at noon that day. So I made some decisions and announcements, hoping senior leaders would support me. Since the Christmas season was coming, I announced publicly that everyone would have a job at a store somewhere in the Des Moines area. Employees did not need to call us—we would be in touch to let them know where to report to get an assignment.

And in the midst of the shock and the grief, there were business matters related to the loss that demanded attention. I tried to reassure family members about company benefits and insurance, and pledged to stay close to them as we learned more.

Staying strong, controlling my emotions, and talking calmly and coherently to families and to members of the press and television in the aftermath of this tragedy was one of the most difficult things I have done in my life. What was clear to me and allowed me to put things in perspective was the knowledge that what I was doing was very hard—but it was nothing compared to losing a loved one. My issues paled in comparison. I was going home to my family.

Monday morning brought new challenges, and the personnel teams from the Merle Hay store and my corporate staff showed up early and we went to work. Where could we locate an employment office? How many people did we employ at Merle Hay? Where could we place them? And what care could we provide to those families?

Fortunately the company was an extremely compassionate employer. We looked after those families, took food gifts, helped children with back-to-school shopping, provided financial support and paid personal visits many times over many years. This was a tragedy of unimaginable loss, and it goes without saying that I wish it had never happened. But the reality is that it did, and I remain profoundly grateful for the way the company handled the tragedy.

When I was in the insurance business more than 70% of the workforce were women. Most were young, at the lower steps of the pay scale, and often they were parents with young children. Many were single mothers, and childcare was a stressful and expensive issue. Since there were many insurance companies in Des Moines, dealing with childcare issues was more of a community issue rather than a single company issue. So I invited human resource leaders from around the community to join in a discussion of how childcare quality and access could be improved. A group of young mothers was invited to share about what problems they were facing and what changes would be most helpful to them. The group made several recommendations, and we implemented them. A database of available licensed childcare providers sorted by zip code was created. This allowed women to shop around and find a convenient location that suited their needs. To be included in the database, licensure and employee training were required. This caused many day care providers to license their operations and upgrade their services. The registry data provided a clear picture of availability (or lack of availability) of childcare in neighborhoods and locations; this saved parents a great deal of time and told us when new providers needed to be recruited. Our model was so successful for all parties—parents, children, childcare providers, employees, employers—that it became a template, and when I was in the Iowa Legislature we passed legislation that expanded those services statewide.

Elected office is public service and a way to give back to the community at large. My thirteen years in the Iowa Legislature provided many opportunities to make a difference—and for that I am grateful. One law that is particularly meaningful to me is the "Safe Haven" law. This law allows a woman who has given birth and sees no way to move forward with parenting to anonymously leave that infant at any health care or law enforcement facility in Iowa, and be confident there will be immediate care and that a good home will be found for that baby. When I first presented the idea, people told me it was just silly, that no woman would follow through and it would serve no purpose. I responded with my usual question: What's the worst that can happen? Answer: We pass the law and no one uses it. No harm, no foul!

The law passed, and since that time I am aware of twenty-two babies (there may be more by now) who have good lives, and twenty-two mothers who found a better alternative for themselves and their babies. The Safe Haven law is a good thing and gives me great satisfaction.

But certainly you don't have to go into public service to give back and pay it forward. Mentoring and coaching one-on-one or in small groups is a fabulous way to make an impact. I enjoy mentoring and coaching people—students, women of all ages, political aspirants who ask to visit with me. The issues they choose to discuss run the full gamut. Parenting, work/life balancing, careers (especially in the Foreign Service or in politics), to run or not to run, even choosing a college major...all life choices worthy of serious consideration. Several times a week I enjoy meeting people for lunch, coffee or a glass of wine to have these conversations. It is rewarding to know that I am respected enough to be asked. I see the remarkable potential in the people I talk to, and watching them act on the things we discuss and achieve the goals they established as a result of our conversation are all wonderfully rewarding outcomes.

At this point in our lives, Kay and I have the luxury of stepping back from the busyness of career and family that filled our time for so many years. The things we pursue now are truly passions. I have returned to my first love of music and serve with great enthusiasm on the board of Des Moines Performing Arts. Working with a fine organization that brings world-class professional performances to Iowans is an unparalleled joy. The mission that brings almost 60,000 children to the Civic Center each year to see and hear live performance is fabulous. Another passion is public media. I try to bring value to the boards of the public television station, to the public television foundation, and to Iowa Public Radio. Public broadcast is one of the few in-depth media voices in our country. Given the biases that exist in so much of our media today, it is absolutely essential to our country that there is at least one media voice available where civil discussion can take place.

Here's one of Kay's favorite ways to give back. From time to time Kay will see a group of uniformed military folk having lunch. He will often tell the waitress he would like to buy their lunch for that day, so bring him their check. Unfailingly, they are overwhelmed as they come to say thank you. And unfailingly, his response is "Thank you for your service."

There are so many ways to give back. Engaging with our community by participating, providing leadership, financial support, time and volunteer energy fulfills our belief that "to whom much is given, much is expected." We have lots to give back because we know we have been given so much! Our experiences living overseas gave us a new appreciation of this fact. Simply being born American is one of the great gifts a person can receive.

KRISTA SAYS:
It's hard to identify a favorite in our list of gems, but if I had to, this might be the one. Nothing has given me more pride and pleasure than to watch the results of "Give Back" at work. I can't recall a

time when this wasn't a priority for any member of my family, starting with stories passed through the generations about my ancestors to the present day, where I can easily list off areas where Kay and Mary, Kent and Kim, my nieces and nephew, and Scott and I are all engaged in giving back.

> *It is one of the beautiful compensations of this life that no man can sincerely try to help another without helping himself.*
> ~ Ralph Waldo Emerson from *The Selected Writings of Ralph Waldo Emerson*

The joy (aka compensation) I feel in my heart, soul and spirit when I am involved in giving back and paying it forward is as beautiful as Emerson describes, and beyond words in some cases. On several occasions I have been moved to tears while giving away $2.00 paperback dictionaries to 3rd graders in Dallas public schools. Often, this dictionary is the first book they have ever owned, and the gentle energy and the thankful spirit of gratitude that fills the school lunchroom where we present the dictionaries is incredible.

Ask my dad about when he played "Taps" on his trumpet at graveside services (some days in the middle of a cold, snowy Iowa winter) to honor our fallen soldiers from World War II and the Korean War. Ask him about the sense of grace and spirit of assisting someone when he drove cancer patients in his limousine to and from the hospital for their chemotherapy or radiation treatments. Ask him about serving meals in elder care homes or with West Des Moines Human Services. Ask him about when he is participating in a recycled bicycle giveaway for kids in the Des Moines area who are receiving a bike for the first time. All you have to do is look on Dad's face and you can see the joy (aka compensation) he is experiencing in helping others. This is the model I have known to follow. You'll understand why my father was honored as a West Des Moines Citizen of the Year. His heart for service is part of his DNA.

Ask my mom about helping a young man in college whose father committed suicide find a summer internship that ultimately shaped his first career and early years of getting established after college graduation.

Ask my husband about mentoring a young man who was incarcerated on a drug conviction, rehabilitated in prison, and who found the Lord. That young man is now devoted to making his community a better place so future young men do not repeat his offenses.

Ask my brother about serving the mission of one of his closest friends who lives as a missionary with his wife and family in rural Africa, where sharing about Christianity is verboten.

Ask my nieces about volunteering at an Indian reservation in South Dakota where they serve children experiencing poverty.

I think the foundation of the sense of service, the heart of service instilled in our family, came from Mary and Kay's rural roots and upbringing. Like most people in their community, they were raised with a spirit of generosity and an inclination to share one's resources—in any way, in whatever amount. I can't count the times my grandmother baked goods for church bake sales or prepared a casserole to take to a family who was grieving or prepared a sandwich tray for the homecoming of a new baby. These simple yet powerful forms of old-fashioned human kindness were just the way things were done. The community as a whole modeled this way of life; this is a great example of living out loud one of our family's most treasured mottos, "To whom much is given, much is expected."

Now, please don't confuse the "much" in "much is given" to mean material things exclusively. This is not the meaning for me, nor for my family. There are plenty of ways to steward our resources—of time, talent, volunteer efforts, or money, no matter how much or how little.

My grandparents on both sides were young married people in the post-Depression era. The Southeast Iowa relatives were educators and farmers, and the Northwest Iowans were educators, farmers, the local butcher, and the grocery store owner. Supplies in their small towns had to last a long time, and everything had to be used and repurposed. Wastefulness was not acceptable. They practiced excellent stewardship of their resources, in other words, and they instilled these values and practices into the successive generations.

Dad has memories of the rationing period during World War II and his dad bringing the bruised produce and "whatever was left in the meat case" home for his mother to find creative ways to prepare. I'm sure many of you can identify with this. Mom has memories of picking vegetables and berries and then participating in days upon days of canning so the family pantries were filled for the winter months. On the family farms everyone had to pitch in—it was just expected—and it brought people together and their shared efforts ensured that each family had enough.

No matter where we lived, Mom and Dad were engaged in volunteer organizations—church, school, parents' groups, community service groups like Rotary International or Altrusa International—or helping out at other service groups like the Kiwanis or the athletic Jaycees supporting the local schools' teams. My dad is the type of man who when he sees the young mother with her hands full in the Hy-Vee parking lot (one kid in her arm, one kid in the car seat, a trunk full of groceries and needing to push her cart over to the cart parking), he'll just step up and say, "Let me get that for you."

Even my grandparents remained engaged in their volunteering, contributing to the betterment of others for as long as they were physically able, which was well into their 80s. My Grandpa Ross would see a neighbor's rose bushes struggling along and go help (even in secret), my grandpa Cyril routinely gave people a ride to the next town or loaned his Buick to someone, my grandmothers would have mini-production factories in their kitchens for breads, rolls and cookies to keep frozen in the event they received a call from "Circle" that there was a need in the community. They took pride in being ready to help if someone was hospitalized, experienced the loss of a loved one, or if there was just any need from a member of the community. They made time for this giving back and paying it forward on a consistent basis, thus enjoying, as Emerson states, "one of life's beautiful compensations."

I truly can't recall a time when I wasn't involved with some kind volunteering or service to others, or being a helper to my mom or dad as a kid while they were engaged in service to others. From grade school, to junior high, to high school–there were a variety of ways students organized as groups to raise funds for extra programs and supplies, band excursions, sports equipment, or special trips. So I would bake some brownies and cookies for the bake sale, participate with a group sale of grapefruit or magazine subscriptions, sell memberships to the boosters or ads on our sports posters and programs. In college my sorority had an annual Volleyball-a-thon and we'd raise money to support the University of Iowa Children's Hospitals.

Early in my professional life, I volunteered with the Young Variety Club and was asked to serve in a leadership role. I was our group's secretary and co-chair for a fundraiser. This role got me mixing and mingling with other young professionals—my first exposure to net-working. Not only did we enjoy serving the Variety Club together, I got to know people and developed professional relationships and built business contacts as a result—this is another version of the "compensa-tion" I think Emerson was referring to.

A really cool pay-it-forward moment in which I was a *recipi-ent* came in 1991. Mom was involved with a very well established networking group, Nexus (the Who's Who of women executives and community leaders in Des Moines). Nexus saw a need for a younger version of their group and decided they'd like to men-tor and seed a similar group of younger professional women. The women who bonded in the late 70's were ready to model the "pay it forward idea" for the women of the early 90's. I lived in Des Moines at this time and was a small business owner. Nexus invited me to join their new group, and it was an excellent place to meet young professional women I wouldn't have otherwise. We called ourselves the Circuit Breakfast Club. Until I relocated to Chicago, I had the privilege of serving as the Secretary/Treasurer. So you see, even the Nexus group of women as an organization identified the value of paying it forward and giving back as a group. I am certain that if tomorrow I picked up the phone or sent an email to any of the members of Nexus, they would respond at their first opportunity, because the kind of women who belong to Nexus believe in these values.

During the year I was transitioning and getting through my divorce, I cannot even express how kind and willing these women were to see me. Some shared their own stories of divorce, some offered suggestions for professional help I could seek out, others shared recommendations for jobs. All were simply willing to listen and act as a fan club to cheer me on to "hang in there" through a rough patch.

After a successful transition to Chicago, I connected with a group of friends in the commercial real estate business who were supporters of the Art Institute. We were all young professionals working hard to make ends meet in the big city, so we didn't have big treasure to donate. But we did have big energy, and we could raise money by giving fabulous parties. I quickly became engaged with the Evening Associates of the Art Institute of Chicago, which is essentially the Institute's under-40 board of professionals who want to make a difference at the museum. It didn't take long to get invited to join their board and become involved with their yearly black-tie. I was honored to co-chair for two years.

During my years getting started as a residential realtor, the company I worked for heavily invested in me despite being 100% commission-based. They had high expectations for production, but in return they backed me up with their time in the roles of coaches, and encouraged mentorship and partnering with well-established agents for real-time experience. No two transactions are the same, so all the experience I could get with those who were willing to invest their time in me was valuable and full of learning opportunities. What a great example of paying it forward and helping your partners in business succeed.

One of the classes they underwrote introduced me to an activity I still use today, Accountability Partnerships. On a weekly basis, two other agents and I shared what we were doing well and where we were challenged and needed help. When we had a success, we examined why the deal went well. When a deal went sour we followed up by examining those circumstances and learning from them. If we were bummed about the deal that didn't happen or even if something in our personal lives wasn't going well, Accountability Partnerships provided us with a space to talk, vent, and be built up. The wisdom and support we gained is invaluable; it made us better at our jobs and more fulfilled in our personal lives. Wouldn't it be terrific for other companies to follow this example?

My husband Scott serves on the leadership team with an organization in West Dallas called 2ndSaturday. 2ndSaturday works to alleviate poverty by way of two distinct platforms. The first is on the second Saturday of every month, a team helps to restore the homes of Senior-Limited-Income-Disabled (SLID) homeowners throughout Dallas's poorest neighborhoods. The second is through working with employers to provide jobs for former gang members, drug dealers, and repeat felons. Scott works side by side with many of these men as a mentor, trusted friend and teacher of new life skills. 2ndSaturday is a local and grassroots organization that is succeeding in disrupting the forces of generational poverty.

Scott's work with 2ndSaturday demonstrates one way we can fill a huge need in our country's culture. What's *your* way of giving back? What are the needs in *your* community—and how can you step up to the plate and pay it forward?

Scott and Ahommed 2ndSaturday 2014

The pièce de résistance in my world where "giving back and pay-ing it forward" are concerned is being a proud Rotarian. Rotary is an international service organization with 1.3 million members—the largest of its kind. Its members come from vastly different countries and cultures, but together we're committed to taking on some of the world's most pressing challenges. It is our shared passion for service that helps us accomplish the remarkable.

For example, beginning in 1979 Rotary Clubs in the Philippines took on a project to raise the finances and resources necessary to immunize six million children. By 1985 the success of this project was so significant that Rotary International launched the worldwide campaign Polio Plus, the first and largest internationally coordinat-ed private-sector support of a public health initiative, with an ini-tial pledge of $120 million. In 1988 there were 125 polio-endemic countries. As I type this today, in August 2014, there are now only three polio-endemic countries.

In Rotary we exchange ideas. Through Rotary my network—and my worldview—is expanded. Rotary brings together great minds from nearly everywhere in the world, and it supports the educational aspirations of thousands of future leaders. Its motto is "Service Above Self."

For me the Rotary principles perfectly align and complement the family principles Mom and I have been sharing throughout the book, especially "to whom much is given, much is expected." So my participation and dedication to Rotary's ideals come naturally to me. Another reason I love Rotary so much is it's a secular, inter-faith organization open to all persons regardless of race, color, creed, religion, gender, or political preference. Rotary brings together business and professional leaders in order to provide humanitarian services, encourage high ethical standards in all vocations, and help build goodwill and peace in the world. What's not to like about that? And we do it locally and globally. It feels awesome to be part of creating lasting change in my local community and around the world.

I believe Rotary models what's very often missing in real community and global leadership. If I can share my life lessons and family principles with my sphere of influence along with Rotary's message, I feel I am making a big impact, not just leaving an impression, and it has a profound ripple effect the more I share.

For You to Say:

- Describe the volunteer experience that has had the most meaning for you. Why?

- What are the areas where you find energy, satisfaction, passion? Can you find volunteer opportunities in these areas?
- What skills or special interests do you (or could you) bring to volunteer groups, associations or charities?

Gem Number Six: Be Patient— But Not Tooooooooo...

Patience is indeed a virtue—but sometimes it is seriously overrated.

MARY SAYS:

In my early years as a piano bar performer, I had a regular Thursday night gig at the American Legion Hall. I would play for several hours and the hall was supposed to close at 10 PM. But some of the older members loved to sing "Old Soldiers Never Die." Later in the evening, they would request that song repeatedly. Often the bartender and the manager would be looking at me with a "time to close" look. I learned that if I just stopped playing and stood up, the gentlemen would be upset and grumble about not getting what they wanted. So instead of the confrontation that made them unhappy, I just kept raising the key of the song. As the pitch kept getting higher, their Adam's apples would begin protruding, their necks stretching a bit, and they would just wear out. Off they went, no one had to confront them about leaving, and they would be back the next week, ready to sing along some more.

When first elected to the Iowa Legislature, I thought the pace was so slow I did not know if I could adjust. During the first several months I was interviewed by a business magazine and asked how I was adjusting to the change from business to politics. I said, "I try not to get outraged more than once a week." After a few months, I began to see the value of having ideas fully vetted. The process by which an idea becomes a law is long and convoluted, but it affirms my belief that no matter how smart one person is, several people working together looking at the issue and reviewing the consequences, both intended and unintended, make for better legislation. That said, with so many competing ideologies and priorities, it becomes necessary to move the process along. Too much patience leads to paralysis.

When I became an Ambassador and met with my country team for the first time, I realized they did not have any cohesive vision of the desired future of our work together. They were all "Lone Rangers" intent on doing their own thing. Their own things were often important and meaningful, but the President had provided a very clear goal: *Maintain Stable Democracies.* It took time, patience and sharing some information about leadership skills, but the country team became an *actual* team. The unifying vision of the desired future became a shared vision. Not because I gave orders or made demands, but because we took the time to envision how each of their individual roles and missions created a win-win situation with the larger Embassy mission.

One of the important jobs of a U.S. Embassy is keeping people back in Washington informed about a variety of things happening in country. Communications (cables) are mostly written by young Foreign Service officers who tend to belabor every word. It is never quite good enough to send. After several document reviews my patience would wear thin. I began going to their work spaces and announcing, "Time to hit print!" Meaning *send it now.* Before long, I walked into a work place and the person at the desk would look up at me and say, "I just hit print, Madame Ambassador."

On the other side of the coin, the more complex the issue or situation, the more valuable patience becomes. This is especially true today when we are calibrated to a "drive-through" mentality. The notion—like television sitcoms—that things can be resolved in thirty minutes has trained us to expect immediate resolutions of problems. Patience requires the judgment to know when to hit print and when to spend time to prepare—to study a problem before making recommendations or moving to action.

As I am privileged to talk with younger people regarding career change, education opportunities, or entering into or determining the importance of relationships, I am struck by the urgent feelings of many that they must "hurry" on to their next step, their next big thing. I remind them to lighten the load. Looking back I realize there are many decades to work, to achieve goals, and to enjoy relationships.

I also believe sometimes patience must take over if one decides to be a parent. There will be many decades to pursue careers, but children have a finite number of years they need the full attention of their parents.

So exercise patience. But don't be toooooo patient!

KRISTA SAYS:

"Our patience will achieve more than our force." Edmund Burke
"Patience is bitter, but its fruit is sweet." Aristotle

The Skills Create Opportunities Gem and the Be Patient Gem often combine nicely for me. I've become adept with practicing patience where most of my relationships are concerned, with my golf game, and other hobbies where skill-building requires repetition, practice and the discipline to stay focused. For years, an especially difficult shot in golf for me was the bunker shot. I would be in the midst of a round, watch an errant shot head for a bunker, and then immediately conclude that my score for the hole, or maybe even the round, was doomed. It took years of practice in the sand and out of the sand and testing out numerous instructions and methods until my body could autopilot into the "get out of here" mindset and send the signal of confidence to my brain. I could do it.

Life does not operate like a fast food drive-through. I've watched over the years and believe we've become an increasingly impatient and antsy society. There's a lot of "I want it now" out there. But patience can be learned—and patience can be a slow teacher. "I want it now" may sound good, but there's also the statement "be careful what you wish for."

Patience is a neat human discipline. I'm proud of the way I have developed my sense and skill of patience over the years; it serves me well in so many parts of my life. Patience can be my imaginary "pause" button in a stressful or rapidly changing situation. It can be the deep breath I take to clear my mind ahead of executing a golf shot, or stepping up in front of a room full of people to speak. Patience is the hope I keep in mind while cooking or baking and waiting for my efforts to turn out as I intend them to. Patience is a quiet place I need to mentally visit when I've grown weary of waiting and want something to happen. Patience also partners beautifully with our Endlessly Pleasant Gem. It also partners well with giving someone the benefit of the doubt—most of the time. I am certain it annoys people who are "I want it now" types—but my patience perseveres.

One of my favorite examples of learning and observing patience comes from my grandfather, Ross Barnett. He was a practitioner of deep breathing to gain calm and clarity well before it became fashionable. I can see him in my mind now, peering through his bifocals, mouth closed, his nostrils flaring as he relaxed, slowed down, and determined his course of action in whatever situation demanded patience. This may have happened while he was reading the newspaper in the morning, or helping me with a puzzle, or putting together a new toy he and Grandma gifted to Kent or me for a birthday or for Christmas. He could've been helping Grandma with her sewing stuff, which often required detailed instructions along with preparing multiple accessories to put together a special pattern she was sewing. He was also a candy maker, and patience is required for the steady, slow process that cannot be abandoned as the cream center of hand-dipped chocolates is "worked" on a marble slab and achieves the proper temperature and consistency for hand-rolling into small balls of filling. The vivid memory of his patient presence and demeanor brings patience to me even 20+ years after he has gone to heaven. I have a Chrysler Imperial Rose bush in our backyard and his spirit of patience lives in those beautiful blooms for me. (A lot of patience and disciplined nurturing is required for the successful livelihood of the Chrysler Imperial Rose bush, so it's only fitting that this serves as one of my symbols for patience.)

My father and my husband are also both patient men. I have an animated personality like my mom, and I am thorough and deliberate like my dad. Mom's and my animated, high energy, "always up for adventures" style often demands patience from Dad and Scott. We're often involved in doing so many things that one leads to or blends right into the next without a significant pause, which can be a challenge to flow with. Scott would tell you he can accomplish 90% of a project in the same time I need to finish 10% of a project. And, my 10% takes place after he has determined his 90% has concluded. Thus, he puts his patience to use with me, because I am very patient while I'm in my thorough and deliberate mode.

My positive attitude may make my patience look easy, but this wasn't always the case. Sometimes my habit of worrying eroded my patience.

As a single woman, home alone in my Chicago condo, I would occasionally sit stewing over various worries in my life. Would that big real estate transaction go through? Would I be able to get out of my self-imposed credit card debt? Would the guy I wanted to go out with call me up and ask me for a date? What should I do when my drive to use my skills to create opportunities didn't align with a prospective employer's timeframe, or an employer's timeframe regarding promotions? (Knowing when to "be patient, but not toooooo" is always a challenge!) My lack of patience put me in some tough emotional spaces on occasion.

It still does, sometimes. When my patience wears thin, I remind myself that this situation is *my* version of tough—there are so many other people who are experiencing an entirely different, worse, and awful version of tough. It's then that I guide myself to an attitude of gratitude, and I follow Grandpa Ross's example in breathing and thinking my way back to a place of calm and clarity. Then, my patience reappears and I stop worrying. I'm kinder to myself, and I can gradually release myself from the bonds of worrying and shift to patiently staying positive. But, I'm here to tell you this takes a lot of practice.

One of the first times that test anxiety didn't cause me to freeze, throw up or freak out was when I took my Illinois real estate salesperson's license exam. I *really* wanted to pass that test. I prepared thoroughly and deliberately, and I strode in to the exam fully confident and calm.

What was the difference? Part of it was that there was something more attached to the outcome of this exam for me. I'd identified a career goal that I really wanted, and I wanted it to go well, to advance me personally and professionally. The other part was patience! I knew I needed to practice the discipline of patience to prepare thoroughly—to put in whatever was required to nail this exam. And I did! With that success under my belt, I began to develop more faith in myself and my abilities to get the job done. Patience with myself and my process made that particular stepping stone possible, and it continues to serve me well today.

Over and over I've learned from my *lack* of patience as well. When it comes to self-improvement, relationships, or my career stops and transitions, a lack of patience means I am not "showing up" or demonstrating my best self, my best me. When I stop and focus on patience as a requirement of success, I succeed. When I first met Scott, our schedules and busy lifestyles with work and friends really challenged me. In the early months, I would get really impatient waiting for him to call to say hi and ask me out. I had determined I would make a point of not pursuing him too much, because I felt like that could be a turn-off. And in previous experience, asking a guy out or suggesting activities too frequently seemed to result in the disappearing guy syndrome. So early on, I would just say to myself, "Just be patient, go about your business, you have plenty to do, there's no need to sit around and wait. Have faith in this relationship, and be patient." And I was right. This level of patience helped me improve independently, and it also demonstrated why having faith in someone I grew to care deeply about was so important to the health of the relationship. Over time, it has matured into what is now my lifelong love.

Krista & Scott Holiday Party Season 2003

For You to Say:

- Describe situations where you have been too patient. How do you recognize cues when patience may be overrated?
- What is your go-to behavior when progress is not happening?
- What are your cues to recognize when patience would improve results?

Gem Number Seven: Mastery is Optional

You can try to master anything and everything—
but you can also change your mind and try
something new.

MARY SAYS:

One of my fondest early memories is of the wonderful old up-right piano that sat in our living room. It must have weighed a thousand pounds. It was very tall, with pillars and ornate carvings in its dark, dark wood. It had a marvelous piano stool that could be adjusted up and down by spinning the top. The bottom of each leg was like an eagle claw, each holding a clear round glass ball. I wish I still had that stool today!

Even before I started to school I could sit at the piano and pick out tunes by ear. I think I was a little "showboat." When I started to school, my parents Ross and Geneva decided I should begin pi-ano lessons. My first teacher, Miss Virginia Dalton, came to school to give those 15-minute weekly lessons. I loved those lessons and I played a sneaky game with Miss Dalton. My first piano book was called "John Thompson's Teaching Little Fingers to Play." At my lesson, I'd ask Miss Dalton to play John Thompson's songs for me, and then I would go home and play them just like she did. Thus I enjoyed immediate success without ever having to practice, and saw no reason to learn to read the notes.

At about this time, my Aunt Ethel began dating my soon-to-be Uncle Ralph, and he became part of extended family gatherings. Since he was a "real" musician and I was an upstart prodigy, I was asked to play for him. I happily complied; I loved showing off. Uncle Ralph was duly impressed but he saw right through my sneaky game. After my first few minutes at the piano he said to Ross, "She plays really well, but did you know she's not reading a note? She's making it up as she goes."

So just like that, Miss Dalton was no more and Uncle Ralph took me under his wing. I began spending Saturday mornings with him in his studio. I listened to his students and heard beautiful music that I loved and wanted to play—music that was far beyond anything I'd found in John Thompson's book. And to play *that* type of music, Uncle Ralph showed me that I must learn to read music. He not only taught me to read the notes, he gave me a reason to do so, and I learned that to play and perform the really great music, the important works by important composers, I not only had to read the notes, I had to practice! That wasn't nearly as much fun as winging it, but I was willing to put in the time to achieve the end result I desired: the ability to perform the gorgeous music that Uncle Ralph had introduced me to.

Mary at the piano 1950

Decades later, I still enjoy playing and it is still more fun and less stressful when I just wing it. If I make mistakes in one of my own arrangements no one knows, but if I make a mistake playing the "Moonlight Sonata" many people know.

During my early years, I was often reminded I had a rare and God-given talent: I could play by ear, something very few people could do. I was also frequently reminded that my talent was a gift. I had done nothing to "earn" this gift, so I had no grounds for pride, cockiness, or bragging. And though I was a natural showboat, showing off was definitely discouraged! Still, receiving applause was (and is) terrific, and I thrive on it. At any rate, after hearing repeated praise about my "rare and God-given talent," by the time I was a teenager I began to worry that my only real value was related to my piano performance ability. My whole self-concept was tied up with piano. What if something happened to my hands? I would be nothing.

Fortunately as I grew older, I accomplished other things and began to realize I had other gifts to share. So even when there is a "gift," mastery is still optional. Through my own choices, the degree of mastery was in my control. I did not have to pour *all* of my efforts into piano playing. I was free to pursue new things, and I'm glad I did.

In seventh grade I could kick the football farther and with more accuracy than any of the boys. I practiced kicking that football until I was the best punter in the seventh grade. I was very proud of this skill and decided I would go out for the team. At that point I quickly learned another lesson about mastery: in this case, no degree of mastery would make me eligible to compete. Girls were simply not allowed to play, and even though my own father was the coach of the team, there was nothing to be done about it. It was so unfair! I then practiced being a very angry and difficult child. I had great mastery of that!

Fortunately, Miss Phyllis McAdam provided the "Y" in the road that allowed me to avoid a long and difficult road of anger and disruption. Miss McAdam was the middle school music teacher. Severely handicapped, she walked with a limp and a cane. That did not diminish her power—the woman was a dictator. It seemed to me she was never in doubt of anything. She selected music that was far too difficult and sophisticated for junior high school students and she decided I would be her accompanist. She demanded near perfect, professional performances—and she got them. This was my first inkling of the discipline required for mastery. Practice does *not* make perfect. Only *perfect* practice makes perfect. The process of joining with others to create excellent performances and the reward of receiving applause for doing so helped me to overcome my anger and made practice fun and rewarding. I had discovered another way to be part of a team and to compete and shine. Part of the joy of accompanying is the satisfaction of being part of a team, of supporting others to make talents shine. Anger is exhausting. Life is too short to stay "stuck." Thankfully, I got over it and moved on.

Ultra-practical Ross and Geneva, who saw no way I could make a career out of piano playing, insisted I take the high school typing course so I would have a job skill. This reflected their belief that I needed a marketable skill I could fall back on in the event that I never got married. So I learned to type. That learning became valuable sooner rather than later and has been an important skill throughout my life.

When I was a sophomore in high school, Ross accepted a job in Iowa City so I could live at home and go to college. It was a way to be sure I could afford college. During my undergraduate years, I lived at home and attended the University of Iowa. I needed a job to pay for tuition and books. My typing skill got me jobs that paid $4.00 an hour. Huge! Most of my friends were earning $1.25 at jobs I really did not want to do. Mastery of typing, while not nearly as satisfying as piano performance, allowed me to earn money for college.

It also taught me that although I quickly mastered this skill, I did not want to be a typist for the rest of my life. Much later, well into my career, I hung a poster in my office picturing Golda Meir, the woman who served as the Prime Minister of Israel. She was sitting at a magnificent desk in a magnificent office. At the bottom of the poster was the question: "But Can She Type?" My fingers can still fly over the keyboard, and I make many mistakes. Thank goodness I can leave the mastery of correcting my mistakes to the computer.

Now one skill I have mastered—at least to the degree I want to—is cooking. I love cooking. Not so much the "what's for dinner tonight?" kind—but producing beautiful dishes for the enjoyment of the people who join us at our dining room table. Geneva, Grandma McElhinney, and all my maternal aunts, "the McElhinney girls," were great cooks. I learned so much just hanging around their kitchens eating the results of their efforts. At one point they had collected over twenty meatloaf recipes. Each a little different combination of meat, seasoning, tomato sauce or juice, saltines or breadcrumbs, etc. One day they got together to have a marathon meatloaf recipe test. The result? A recipe they officially designated as "This Is It Meatloaf." And it is!

The McElhinney Girls circa 1970's

Cooking is one of the great traditions in our family. I think Krista is a better cook than I am at this point, much more adventurous and contemporary. Because we talk about food so much, we will share some of the most beloved recipes and their stories at the end of the book. You will find the recipe for "This Is It Meatloaf" is the Big Plates Section.

Now let me tell you where I lean *heavily* on the Mastery is Optional gem. Early in our marriage, I realized that Kay *loved* golf. It seemed like a great way for us to spend time together and a great game for us to enjoy together—but I had never played. So on our first anniversary Kay gave me golf clubs and I took up the game. I had a golf game that was "acceptable." Not great, but not embarrassing. I could compete in events and even win from time to time—but my game certainly wasn't masterful! That was beside the point. The point was, I loved the game, Kay and I enjoyed playing together, and we developed a lovely social life around the game of golf. That's a win-win for everyone.

During the busy parenting and career years, time to play golf disappeared. Later, when I tried to return to the game, I found I had gone from acceptable to awful. I blamed it on several things: all the golf genes went to the kids, too many years without playing, a bad hip, a worse attitude. Whatever the cause, any skill I had was long gone. Today my game is still awful but I invoke the "Mastery is Optional" gem and just enjoy playing. It is great to spend time enjoying beautiful golf courses with friends and family. I choose my playing partners and my outings carefully because I prefer not to keep score and I play by Mary's rules. When you play by Mary's rules you never have to hit your ball out of a sand trap—that's why there are rakes. I never mastered the game because I was not willing to take lessons and practice to improve. I just wanted to have fun and spend time with people I love. Plus I always *believe* my next shot will be great. Unfortunately my body doesn't seem to be able to follow what my brain is visualizing. It's a humbling game and it provides me with all the humility I can handle. Thank goodness Kay enjoys golf so much he will still play with me.

KRISTA SAYS:

Well Mom is correct: She did give up her golf genes during pregnancy and passed them along to my brother Kent and to me! (Insert laughter here, please.) We started playing about the time we each turned five. Each of us had some great re-purposed clubs procured by Dad through keen garage-sale shopping. As I recall, mine was a cut-off Spaulding 4-wood wrapped with red electric tape for the grip, while Kent started with a 5-wood and his was wrapped in black tape.

Circa the early 70's, we were living in Iowa City and there were two golf courses where kids could play along with parents if they remained sensitive to the pace of play. Initially I used whiffle balls and Kent used hand-me-down or re-claimed pond balls from Dad or our grandpas. At some point we had lessons from the Quail Creek pro, J.D. Turner. (He later became my first employer at Des Moines Golf and Country Club.) We were shown the basics—grip, alignment, set-up, and basic swing motions—and then off we went to play.

What happened? We fell in love with golf. We knew this was a skill we wanted to master, and we put in the time and the hours. Kent and I both excelled as junior players.

Golf was a huge part of our lives and still is today. We watched golf on TV, read *GOLF Magazine*, *Golf Digest*, and here and there had occasional lessons from different pros. We played often as a family, and family spring break trips were always to a golf destination for the purpose of playing golf at special courses.

Krista high school senior picture 1984

I loved golf so much that I wanted to master it, maybe even make a career out of it. My career in professional golf is one of the chapters in my life where the Mastery is Optional Gem couldn't be more evident.

One part of the final requirements for my college degree program was to log 100 hours of work and complete an internship at a recreation-related facility where I could potentially work following graduation. At that time, J.D. Turner, the professional who'd first shown Kent and me the basics of the golf swing in the early 70's, was the Director of Golf at Des Moines Golf and Country Club. Let's just stop and give my Dad credit for keeping track of the success stories in the Iowa golf world. He suggested I consider applying for a summer job in the golf shop and asking to intern there. Like Dad, J.D. is a huge supporter of University of Iowa athletics and alums. So Dad made an appointment for us to pay a visit to J.D. I hardly recall the details of the meeting, but it must have gone well because J.D. said yes to my request for an internship without hesitation.

I started in the golf shop during my summer break in 1988, completed my final semester of courses that fall, and my internship took place during the second semester of the 1988-89 school year. Now fast-forward to the spring of 1989, when graduation was just around the corner. The internship had gone so well that I was offered a permanent position with Des Moines Golf after graduation and was made an Assistant Professional on staff. For the next two years I dedicated myself to the golf profession and worked on it from sunup to sundown: I was on a pursuit of full mastery. I played well enough to get my handicap to a 4—from the men's tees. I complained sometimes about the difficulty and unfairness of this, and Mom was always quick with her reply: "Life is played from the men's tees, get over it."

In my full-time role, I was responsible for purchasing the golf shop merchandise and ordering nearly all of the many items necessary to operate a world-class golf facility. I enjoyed great relationships with my bosses, peers and the members of Des Moines Golf and Country Club. I entered the PGA Apprentice Program. I knew I could be a performance-quality competitive player and successful teaching professional...if I wanted to. Key phrase: *if I wanted to*. At twenty-something, fresh out of college, I had just started to realize that my professional "I want to" was only the first of *many* desires in life.

I was taught to be grateful for my God-given talents, abilities, instincts and gifts, and I was. But I was always asking myself, "How long will you stay in the golf business? What is your career path? Do you want to be a head pro somewhere? Do you want your own gig some day? How can you save the cash to afford it?" Looking back now, I'm guessing I was afraid to commit to the "I want to, and I'll do whatever it takes" to be a professional golfer. Frankly, I don't believe I was mature enough to commit—I was very young and there was a world of choices available to me.

Still, I'd invested a great deal of time and effort in my endeavor to become a professional. I'd immersed myself in everything I could about the club operations, from the study of teaching the game, to running tournaments, to keeping track of merchandise, to repairing clubs, and even on down to learning about turf grass. Oh yes, and being accepted into the PGA's apprentice program required passing their specialized vocational training called "Business School," which also required me to pass a four-hour multiple-choice exam, and I had huge test anxiety. I needed two tries to get that first one accomplished, but I persevered. And although I was burning out on golf, I still attempted to pass the Player's Ability Test (36 holes in one day with a target score to beat). I think I tried four, five, maybe even six times.

So what ultimately happened? The "playing and practicing" of golf, the business of the sport, and my level of dedication to all things golf—in short, my pursuit of mastery—actually brought me to a place where I made the decision *not* to pursue "mastery." At that time, I defined mastery as getting the Class A Professional designation. But guess what I discovered? The business side and the relationships with the members were much more attractive, motivating and meaningful to me. I had learned, in other words, that Mastery is Optional, and that I was free to change my mind at any time and try something new.

And it was in trying something new that I discovered what brought me true meaning and joy, and paved the way for every other fulfilling decision I've ever made.

For You to Say:

- What are some things you have mastered? What are some things you've tried and decided weren't for you? What did you learn from both experiences?
- What are some things you would like to master? Put another way, what are the things you feel would help you become a better person, a better employee, a better parent?
- What's stopping you from trying new things or from reaching toward mastery?
- How can you remove those barriers?

Gem Number Eight: Endlessly Pleasant

*We demean others by cursing, using sarcasm,
cynicism or put-downs.
We diminish ourselves and our effectiveness as well.*

MARY SAYS:

My earliest language lesson came at Grandma McElhinney's Sunday dinner table. Family gatherings were a large group with multiple generations and aunts, uncles and cousins. Sunday dinner was fabulous. There was always fried chicken, mashed potatoes and gravy, home-canned vegetables, ten kinds of Jell-o, and a variety of pies.

There were also fascinating discussions. The entire family was Republican, and the only differential was the degree of conservatism. During the presidential race between Harry S. Truman and Thomas Dewey, I was about five years old. On the way home from school, I had seen graffiti on a fence that said "Shit on Dewey." Feeling very proud and grownup, I felt I had something to contribute to the discussion, so at the Sunday dinner table I piped up and said, "*Shit on Dewey!*" There were horrified gasps followed by a prolonged silence. Once he recovered, my father Ross grabbed my hand and marched me to the bathroom. The taste of soap in my mouth was so disagreeable I can still taste it. That was my first lesson in learning that words really have consequences. I had shocked and disappointed everyone at the table—all the people who were most dear to me. From that day forward the s-word has never been a part of my vocabulary.

Ross was my most positive role model for remaining calm and pleasant. I never saw him lose his temper. Like everyone he could be angry, and I knew when he was angry and I knew there would be consequences. But he calmly let me know what he was angry about. There was never shouting, name-calling, or hurtful personal attacks. I sincerely admire that model. I try, but I have never quite lived up to his example. A little too much Irish in my temperament, perhaps.

Thoughtful speech and measured responses, and practicing kindness and civility, is what I call Endlessly Pleasant. It requires great discipline on my part. But it's worth it every time. I have learned that focusing on issues and not personalities *always* leads to better outcomes—broader participation, more problems solved, an agenda advanced, fewer hurt feelings, and an increased likelihood that promised follow-up will take place. In contrast, any time the principle of Endlessly Pleasant isn't in play, I've witnessed hurt feelings, jeopardized initiatives, and an undermining of any team effort, not to mention general inefficiency.

Howard Schultz, founder and CEO of Starbucks says, "I realize that idealism is out of sync with the cynicism of our era. Skepticism has become synonymous with sophistication and glibness mistaken for intelligence. In such an atmosphere, why bother aiming high? I just want to reassure people to have the courage to persevere, to keep following their hearts even when others scoff. Don't be beaten down by naysayers. Don't let the odds scare you from even trying." This is Endlessly Pleasant at its best.

Immediately after I was elected the President of the Iowa Senate I met with members of the media in the Capitol Rotunda. One reporter said to me, "What are you doing here?" I told him I had just been elected the President of the Senate. He said, "NO way! You're female, moderate and urban—three strikes and you're out." The newly appointed minority leader said to me, "I like you, but it is now my job to make your life miserable." I answered, "You are not capable of doing that unless I let you—and I won't be doing that."

When we have a shared goal of being effective and of making a difference, then remaining civil and Endlessly Pleasant is a reliable way of keeping an agenda moving and helping people to stay on point. It may be easier to just go along, to follow the example of late night talk show hosts as they deliver monologues that are simply a collection of "put-downs," but it is just not effective. Habitually taking cheap shots while the audience laughs at the expense of someone else is not the model of a person who wants to help make things better.

Endlessly Pleasant should never be mistaken for being a pushover. Like Ross, you can be firm in your opinions and make sure your message is crystal clear without having to resort to the low blows of shouting, name-calling, and insults.

KRISTA SAYS:
The skills involved in remaining Endlessly Pleasant have been demonstrated to me in numerous venues throughout my life.

Golfers who absolutely come unraveled when they're playing poorly, cursing and throwing their clubs, don't realize how much Endlessly Pleasant is needed, especially in a competitive round. From my own personal learnings about getting mad or upset during a round, I've come to value being Endlessly Pleasant with myself while playing golf. This might even translate to being forgiving toward myself when I have a poor shot, or I play a round that just isn't my best. It happens.

Turn on the Golf Channel, watch any of the tours and you'll see the proof that the principle of Endlessly Pleasant works. Golfers who retain their equanimity no matter what and let the "rub of the green" simply happen with an accepting attitude play better, enjoy the game more, and thrive more in competition. You'll hear pros say over and over during interviews after winning tournaments, "I just knew I had to trust my game and trust my plan." For the player who loses sight of their internal trust system the game only gets worse—not only for the player but for everyone around them.

In high school and college, I would sometimes caddie for friends when they played competitively. One summer during a City of Des Moines boys' junior tournament at Waveland Golf Course, a player came completely unglued on a Par 3 and launched his pitching wedge into the air. I still remember the sound of the whirling club—like spinning helicopter blades—as it sailed high over a metal chain fence and outside the course boundaries. Fortunately it landed in an area where there were no people, but unfortunately, we couldn't retrieve the wedge without causing a major delay for the playing group. After this failure of Endlessly Pleasant and the player's display of poor sportsmanship, the positive temperament of the threesome competing completely disappeared. I almost left him to his misery and alone out there to carry that bag all by himself, but that wouldn't have been Endlessly Pleasant, now would it? After we made the turn to the back nine, this incident was still eating away at him so badly that he stuck his head under the water spigot, shook out his wet hair, dried off and apologized to his fellow competitors and to me. Once the temperament of Endlessly Pleasant was restored, we were all able to have a laugh about the helicopter sound of the spinning club, and we all stepped off the next tee box and managed to salvage the round.

While serving as my Rotary club's president, I had to call upon my Endlessly Pleasant skills quite frequently. One person in particular really tested me, and I'm grateful for the thicker skin I developed as a result. Everyone in the club was a target for this person's constant sarcasm and mean-spirited "gotcha" attempts. An incompetence to be pointed out, a failure of follow-up, a missed opportunity—you name it, this person had a complaint about it. One time when I was the target of these actions, I decided it was time to let it be known that my leadership style wasn't built that way, and that public outbursts as well as group email complaints and diatribes weren't going to work. I started my email response as follows: "I need to know about your concerns, especially when you are displeased with me as the leader, but we're going to have a very long year if you keep up your complaining in its current hurtful form and don't modify your methods of expressing your displeasure about me or other members."

Over and over I attempted an effective use of Endlessly Pleasant. I remained lighthearted, and listened carefully to the person's complaints without taking them to heart. When a person is that consistently negative there's almost always a deeper issue at work than the surface-level "complaint du jour." In this case, with time and a consistent use of an Endlessly Pleasant persona in my interactions with the person, the mean-spirited commentary gradually diminished.

I've certainly noticed the presence—and absence—of the principle of Endlessly Pleasant in the business world as well. It seems that some employees in the decades between my mother and me want to do all they can to prevent a younger employee from moving up the ladder. They demand that everyone "pay your dues like I did." This is an absolute failure at the Endlessly Pleasant principle. They seem to be unable to evolve or facilitate a positive change in the process of professional growth simply because they believe they had difficult and unfair experiences. In their minds, the younger person should suck it up and experience the same unfair and difficult times—and surmount them if they're any good, or fail if they're not. This is totally the opposite of Endlessly Pleasant and it's unproductive for the younger person trying to make it as well as for the people around them. A failed strategy all around.

Once when I was in the commercial real estate business, a major lease negotiation was going on between our company, representing the Landlord, and the prospective Lessee and their Tenant Broker and Attorneys. Our spokesperson entered the room and complimented the Tenant Representative on her beautiful navy suit. She replied, "This is my don't f--- with me suit." Right then and there, the tone and mood was established. Everyone in the room knew how that lease negotiation meeting was going to go. And sure enough, it was unpleasant and unproductive for everyone. A lose/lose deal.

As you might have guessed, I couldn't resist calling Mom and telling her about this incident. Not that a few cuss words haven't ever escaped my mouth, but I do have a filter, and I try and abide by the "right time, right place" judgment call about what I say. (Otherwise known as the "think before you speak" rule. You can't take it back once it leaves your mouth, after all.)

Mom was not surprised by the woman's comment or the ensuing tone the meeting. "Graciousness and courteousness are always winners in challenging moments," she reminded me, and encouraged me not to give one more thought to the potential effectiveness of this woman's style.

She was right. Even if it had been effective in the short term, it wouldn't be in the long term. More importantly, it was simply not how I wanted to comport myself in a business or a personal environment. Endlessly Pleasant allows you to maintain your integrity, interact favorably with others, and get the results you want. It *works*. And I'll stand up for that any day.

For You to Say:

- Describe situations when you practiced or observed outcomes of Endlessly Pleasant.
- Have there been situations in your experience where Endlessly Pleasant might have changed the tone of a meeting or conversation to achieve a better outcome?
- Can you imagine situations in your life where Endlessly Pleasant could be helpful?

Gem Number Nine: Assertiveness is Not Optional

Being assertive requires one to have an opinion,
the courage to speak, the discipline to stay on point,
and the willingness to engage in civil discussion
with those who disagree.

MARY SAYS:

My first teaching job included working with classroom teachers who were expected to teach music to their own class. At that time there was no elementary music teacher, so the job of teaching music twice a week fell to classroom teachers who didn't necessarily have a background in music. Part of my job was to develop lesson plans and do demonstration classes each week. Of course I was the rookie and nearly all the teachers I was working with had at least five years of experience. Some had over 20 years of experience and I could tell it had been the same year 20 times! They wondered—often aloud—what I thought I could teach them.

How could we get to a win-win situation? My solution was to make the demonstration lesson plan so clear it would be easy for everyone to follow, and so enjoyable for the kids they would be eager for their next music class. When the kids looked forward to it, it would be very difficult for the teacher to avoid doing it. By making my demonstration classes simple for the teacher and fun for the students, there was opportunity for kids to have a music class at least once a week, even though there was no designated music teacher. I didn't allow myself to be intimidated or silenced by the veterans, and we moved forward together with a program that worked for everyone. Assertiveness involves the ability to use influence without resorting to win/lose strategies.

During my years in retail it became apparent that women merchants needed some assistance in asserting themselves in ways that led to successful negotiations, problem solving, and achieving desired outcomes. The ability to communicate without being perceived as overly aggressive (not to say bitchy) was paramount. At the time, women were just beginning to move into positions of leadership, particularly in merchandising. They were given an opportunity because they had great fashion sense, innate marketing skills, and knew their customers. However, they did not have leadership experience or negotiation skills. The textile industry was moving to Asia, so a spirit of independence that included solo international travel and competency in negotiation became a necessary part of their skill set. I suggested they be given the opportunity to experience what was then called "Assertiveness Training." I planned to take the classes myself to assure that the content and quality met our expectations. During a meeting to discuss this idea, one of the officers attempted a joke: "Absolutely not. We do not need *you* to become any more assertive. This company does not need any more Mary Kramers!" I told him that I took that as a compliment and moved on.

Later on I had a measure of our success. One of our young women buyers was in a New York hotel elevator when a man exposed himself. Instead of panicking, she looked him in the eye and said, "So, is that it?" and got off on the next floor. *Assertiveness at its best.*

As the President of the Iowa Senate, there were many times when I realized I was not going to change ideas and beliefs. While presiding in the Senate Chamber, I sat in the huge black leather tufted chair (I had to have a box under my feet or they did not touch the floor). The desk was raised four steps above floor level. Behind me were several flags and two "guest chairs." The voting board was on one side and a smaller desk sat on the other.

Mary Presiding Over Iowa Senate Session 1998

Those desks on either side were staffed by pages. Pages were high school seniors who received school credits to come to the Capitol in Des Moines and work during the legislative session for six to eight weeks. The Iowa Senate has a great tradition of decorum with very specific rules on protocol and procedure during floor debate. Usually those rules worked well. But sometimes in the heat of debate, a senator would forget protocol. So when name-calling began, or accusations of "political" gains started to fly, I would hit the gavel and remind the speakers of "Rule 23." Rule 23 expressly forbade questioning the motives of another Senator. That would usually be sufficient to change the tone, but early in my tenure, one of my colleagues was unable to contain himself. After the third gavel, I asked him to approach the front of the chamber. He was a little sheepish by the time he arrived and said, "I guess I overdid it a little." I smiled at him and said, "Yes, and not just a little. If it happens again, you will leave me no choice but to refuse to recognize you in the future. Neither of us wants that." He agreed. I asked him to step back and he returned to his seat. The Page beside me leaned over and whispered, "Wow! Chicks rule!" I've often thought since that that would make a great bumper sticker.

That little scene provides us with a great metaphor on assertiveness: When one is given the gavel, she must be willing to use it. It is not realistic to expect passionate people to change their opinions or their beliefs. Decorum can be maintained by politely steering the way people express themselves in debate (or disciplining them if necessary), not trying to persuade them to change their beliefs. And always with a laser focus on the rule or the issue, not on the person.

During my tenure as a U.S. Ambassador, I read and heard remarks from one of the Prime Ministers of my countries calling the U.S. Secretary of State a liar. He might have used different words, but there was do doubt of his meaning, and his remarks were offensive. I called him on the telephone and told him I was unhappy with his remarks, and if his words were an accurate description of his feelings toward our Secretary of State and our country, I was going to have a very difficult time working with him in the future. He immediately became contrite and started to backpedal—certainly he was misquoted, he assured me, and the words I had heard were taken out of context. But I knew better. I remained formal and closed our conversation almost immediately. "I heard your speech on the radio, Sir, and I think I understood perfectly." Two days later he called back and invited his "sister from Iowa" and her husband to come to his country and spend a weekend with him and his wife so he could make it clear how much he respected the USA. I don't think so! Somehow our schedule never allowed us to accept his invitations.

An example of assertiveness that gives me great satisfaction is helping a young Haitian boy join a family in the United States. A birth date was a requirement for a visa, and he had no birth records. We could not determine how old he was. Family consent was required for a child to leave the country. There was a kind woman he called grandmother who looked after him, but he wasn't sure if he was actually related to her. At the time we began the process, he had fallen and broken his leg and was in a bed in a dirty orphanage with his leg in traction, which consisted of a trapeze gadget weighted down by a paint bucket.

The pastor of Scott's parents' church and his wife, who been to Haiti on a mission trip, were convinced they should adopt this young boy and had tried every possible way to get him a visa to come to the U.S. and live with their family. Haiti was so corrupt at that time there was virtually no government to help, and since the boy had no documentation of any sort, our consulate was unwilling to take a chance.

When Krista called to ask me if I could help, I agreed to investigate what was going on there. Everyone of my colleagues I spoke to told me it was a no-win situation and that I should leave it alone. It was just too big a risk for me to intervene.

But I had such a potent visual of this youngster lying in the orphanage in pain. I just couldn't let it go. So I went up the chain of command until I finally got someone in consular affairs to listen.

Wilky was finally issued a visa and came home to Wisconsin. Today he has graduated high school, been to college, and is a bright and healthy young adult who gives back to his native country. He raises money and returns to Haiti with teams of people who build houses. What a great success story he is. He and his adopted parents are to be celebrated!

Deby, David & Wikly Clark, Krista, Kay and Mary 2006

A simple but effective tactic that demonstrates assertiveness is to ask questions as a method of clarification. One question that gets to the heart of the issue is *"What problem are we trying to solve?"* I found this to be particularly useful in politics. When discussing proposed legislation with amendments flying, often not germane to the topic, that question was very effective in keeping us on point. When discussion is heated and voices are raised, ask a clarifying question even if you think you know the answer. You can restate the person's answer and seek confirmation: "This is what I thought you said…" and then paraphrase the comments. Follow with "Am I correct?" This method is nonjudgmental and does not take sides—and it ensures that you speak up. You lack integrity when you leave a meeting or end a conversation without expressing yourself, only to complain to others about the outcome afterward. Asserting oneself is always a better alternative than being a sideline whiner. Grandma McElhinney, that wise woman, often said, "When there is no solution we must seek it lovingly." Years later I learned Socrates said something similar. Grandma McElhinney was even wiser than I thought.

Being assertive also means being willing to "Raise Your Hand." Is someone seeking a volunteer leader? Is there an opportunity to run for office? If you are offered a promotion—even if it requires a move or you feel unqualified—ask for time to consider it. Do not just say no. When presented with a career opportunity at a company that was considered a terrible place to work, when asked to run for office, when invited to become a U.S. Ambassador…each opportunity came with risks and each required a thoughtful response, but in each case after thoughtful consideration I raised my hand and said yes.

KRISTA SAYS:
Full disclosure: For me assertiveness has required lots of practice and it is still required today. I will also disclose that assertiveness for me aligns with my perceived level of accomplishments or state of confidence at any given time. For example, on the golf course,

I am comfortable and confident. Golf has been a great teacher of assertiveness and a place to practice it regularly. I've needed to assert myself in situations where a rules breach and penalty was in question. It's not easy to interrupt the flow of the playing group to inquire about a score re-count, or a penalty confirmation. (I *almost* started typing, "for women especially," but it's true across the board, as the rules of golf are numerous and complex.) In my case, when I've played with a group of guys and I am clearly the player who is most "in the know" about the rules, often with the highest skill level or the most experience, assertiveness is necessary for pace of play, sportsmanship, and keeping the group's mojo on the positive side.

Because golf still remains a male-dominated sport, we women have to be assertive together as well as independently in the golf environment (and spaces like it). So often I have watched a beginner woman or junior golfer have a meltdown due to some "know it all" player or a course staff person voicing their impatience with a beginner's inexperience. When I see this kind of rude, impatient behavior toward women or juniors at the golf course, it's a test of my ability to remain Endlessly Pleasant. It *really* bugs me. (Another full disclosure: I did at one time hit balls back toward foursomes who would hit into my group inappropriately. At times I enjoy pushing the Endlessly Pleasant envelope!)

My confidence about golf and my ability to play came in handy during the years I worked in the mainly men's world of commercial real estate during the late 90's. It helped to balance the gender gap and my game added to my credibility. After it became known I had a game, I received many invitations to participate in charity events and tournaments. I was often on the winning team. This gave me exposure to many people, opened many doors and created many useful networking opportunities.

I'm "wired for thoroughness." I observed and learned about thoroughness from both my parents and my Grandpa Ross, too. Consequently, this desire for thoroughness also aligns with high expectations and slowly developing confidence on my part. I've had to learn that even if in my mind I do not have all the information or knowledge in a given situation, to feel wholly confident I must still be ready to respond and be assertive. This is still a challenge for me, but I've improved greatly over the years.

As with any skill you want to be good at and feel confident about, practice is required. Developing assertiveness isn't part of our human autopilot, so we have to learn, we have to be taught, and we have to identify the model of behavior we feel good about. And the need for assertiveness can more often than not sneak up on you. For example, being put on the spot and needing to respond assertively and confidently, versus having some time to prepare to be assertive and to decide to be assertive with confidence. In my world, my physical skills of golf and playing the piano created the opportunities for me to develop confidence, yet this confidence was the kind that didn't require me to open my mouth and speak up. The confidence to talk or not talk with assertiveness has been a longer, more thorough development journey for me.

Over time and as I matured, one of the best verbal assertions I've become comfortable with is acknowledging what I don't know. An example comes from my years in commercial real estate, when showing prospective tenants vacant spaces in older buildings. There's a dramatic difference in construction methods and building codes over the years. As the leasing agent, I couldn't be expected to know every last detail of what was in the walls, above the ceiling from a wiring or cabling capacity, even ventilation, or asbestos, or fire protection, could I? Unless I'd been with the building since it came out of the ground and on site during every phase of build-out, I wouldn't have all the historical, technically important information. Even as I became acquainted with reading build-out drawings and electrical plans, inevitably there were simply many details about old build-out I did not know, or even the building engineers did not know. I learned over and over to simply look the prospective Tenant in the eye and tell her or him I did not know everything hidden behind the walls, under the floors and overhead above the ceilings in each vacant space. There is only so much we can verify until some demolition gets started. And, because there were always some savvy Tenant Representatives and Brokers who wanted to catch me confirming something that wasn't there, such as implying there was a certain level of cabling in the building conduit leading to that specific space, getting comfortable with an assertive "I don't know" became an important, non-optional part of this skill.

A favorite "what I do know" assertiveness moment occurred when I was sitting in church with Scott's family and heard their pastor's wife, Debi Clark, talk about her yearning to adopt a young Haitian boy, Wilky. This was in December 2003, right after Mom had been confirmed by the Senate Foreign Relations Committee to be ambassador to Barbados. I knew from conversations with Mom that she would be working with Meg, a career diplomatic corps member with extensive experience in Haiti.

Later that summer, after Mom had been sworn in, Scott's mom Kathy called and asked if I felt comfortable getting in touch with Mom and Meg to ask for help with the Wilky adoption situation, which was going nowhere in a hurry because of Wilky's unknown age and likely the corruption associated with adoptions. We immediately got David and Debi Clark in touch with Mom via emails and phone calls, and the process started moving along again. When some bumps in the road occurred, Mom asked me to confirm that this was important to me, and that I wanted her to move up the food chain and rattle some of those chains. I confirmed that yes, this was a situation where I knew we could make a difference. Without going into all the details of the ensuing process, I'll just say that Wilky's adoption and return to the States with the Clarks was a down-to-the-wire, life-changing event, and there were some very stressful moments involved--not the least of which was a government coup on the very day Wilky was to leave! But thanks to being able to "raise my hand" and rely on my heart to be assertive in this instance, I was able to play a role in uniting Wilky with his adoptive family. I'm still beyond thrilled with the outcome, and I still share a special connection with the Clarks thanks to our experience together.

Assertiveness as a key, intentional, "be ready to speak when it's your turn" skill never became more apparent than after we moved to Dallas and the reality of not knowing a lot of people was staring me in the face. Remember, I moved to Chicago with a circle of friends built in, and I landed my first job in Chicago because of who I knew. After 14 years of living and working in Chicago, I had a great "Rolodex" and the blessing of many loyal, established friendships and professional peers. In Dallas, not so much.

It wasn't until I found myself on track with She Kan! Kompany and coaching as my chosen profession in Dallas that I returned to working on assertiveness. As an entrepreneur, my first step into assertiveness was to be out and in front of people, sharing my 30-second elevator speech in front of large networking groups. You didn't know I was pretty terrified of speaking in public until now, did you? I just *dreaded* it when the rapid-fire 30-second spotlight was on me. Some groups have timers, and sound a bell or buzzer when 30 seconds are up. In my case, to this day if I'm not done and the bell goes off, I often lose track of my concluding thoughts, and sit down feeling disappointed in myself. This felt like "the death of me" in the beginning. But…I persevered, and a sense of humor helps enormously. Public speaking is still not my favorite part of networking, but just as the Marines train people to adapt and overcome, so must I adapt and overcome in networking.

Krista Presenting Her Strategizing for Success Message 2013

The next part of adapting to a more comfortable level of acceptance where assertiveness is concerned came when I began to receive invitations to be a speaker. People were becoming friends, getting to know me, meeting Scott, learning about us, and wanting to know more. Flattery like this is a big confidence booster. It's confidence-building to be wanted and invited. It feels good. But me, a speaker? You want me to come and talk to a room full of people about my coaching? About my life story? Golf? Being the kid of an Ambassador? How I help people? *What?!*

Well, thank goodness for Rotary leadership training. Thank goodness for leadership opportunities in volunteer organizations. Thank goodness that other entrepreneurs in my networking groups also struggle with the assertiveness needed to muster up the confidence to speak publicly for more than 30 seconds. Scott, who's been with me throughout this entire process, will proudly tell you that he is delighted with the public speaking and leading skills I've developed as a result of joining Rotary, other organizations and networking like crazy. Thanks to networking and volunteer leadership in Dallas, my confidence has been boosted. I have improved in the "ready to respond" assertiveness department tremendously.

Assertiveness can certainly feel risky in certain circumstances, so I encourage you to explore your appetite for risk and be as prepared as possible. Use another skill you feel confident about to lean on as you develop your assertiveness style like I have with golf. I've also watched and learned from many different experiences with Mom, as well as many other people over the years. Be willing to learn. Be willing to be coached about assertiveness and practice. Identify more than one person you can adapt and model your assertiveness behavior style from. Get comfortable with a level of assertiveness that serves you with significance today and work to develop it more and more over time. Give yourself permission to at any given moment confidently take risks speaking up, not only as a responder but as the person in the front of the room who chooses to speak assertively and enjoys it.

For You to Say:

- Can you describe people who are effectively assertive?
- Do you view yourself as appropriately assertive?
- Do you recognize opportunities where asserting yourself could lead to better outcomes?
- Can you describe a situation where you used clarifying questions?

Gem Number Ten: Lighten Up

"A sense of humor is just common sense, dancing."
~William James

MARY SAYS:

Shortly after Kay and I were married, our parents became friends. They enjoyed trips together, usually to visit us or for all of us to visit a city together. Those trips always included shopping. Here's how it went: The "girls" (Wilma, Geneva and I) would head to the stores. The "boys" (Ross, Cyril and Kay) would head to the nearest bar. Wilma and Geneva did not approve of drinking and they never acknowledged that their boys enjoyed having an adult beverage from time to time. We would set a time to meet in neutral territory. If the "boys" were a little tardy I volunteered to find them. This was not difficult since I knew exactly where they would be. This system worked perfectly for many years. No one had to acknowledge behavior they didn't like and everyone enjoyed the outings.

While I was serving as the Assistant Superintendent in Iowa City, the topic of "family life education" (a euphemism for sex education) became heated and caused some real disagreements in the schools and throughout the community. School board meetings became circuses with overflow crowds and many people wishing to publicly express their opinions—not always politely. Since elementary education was my responsibility, I was asked to discuss this controversial curriculum in the elementary schools at a school board meeting. I began my remarks by saying: "I'm pleased to discuss this curriculum with you this evening. It has been carefully researched and the expected learning outcomes will be measured with just as much care. But I confess, I have some concern about this whole topic." The room suddenly became perfectly quiet. Where was I going with this? "This curriculum and this topic are important and well presented," I continued, "but I fear we in education might make it as boring as reading." The room burst into laughter and I moved on with an audience that wasn't so defensive and was prepared to listen.

Months after a disastrous first interview with the retail company, my first day on the job finally arrived, and I was more than a little concerned about what to wear. After all, this was a fashion business. I chose a white silk blouse, black slacks and black pumps, and a well-cut, bright red blazer. I thought I looked very businesslike. I was met at the employee entrance by an employee from Personnel who greeted me warmly and conducted me to my office. It was a lovely room. She handed me my name badge and informed me I was expected to attend the weekly merchandise meeting in the President's office in fifteen minutes. As I walked into the room, the other officers (all men) were sitting on the window seats, or in those beautiful black leather and chrome chairs. Of course they all stood when I came into the room, and I got a great look at their attire. Every last one of them wore an elegant dark suit, a white shirt, a subdued necktie, and highly polished black shoes. I glanced around the room and said, "Who died?"

Some of those men appreciated my humor and laughed, but others gave me and one another looks that said, "I knew it was a mistake to hire a woman." From that moment on, I knew who was going to be a colleague and who was not.

I was asked to introduce the Governor at my Rotary Club meeting. This was my club, the 300-member *senior* group. I was seated on the podium with the Governor. I hung my purse with my cell phone in it on the back of my chair—neglecting to turn it off. As I was making my remarks at the podium, my phone rang. I just looked around as if I was bit annoyed and gave a little shrug as if to say "*Whose phone is that?*" and kept on with my introduction. After the meeting several of my friends remarked that the inopportune ring sounded like my phone. I blinked innocently and said, "Really, did you think so?"

On a lovely warm day in early spring I was delivering the keynote address at a very well attended women's conference. I was sitting at the piano using music to illustrate and reinforce my points. Suddenly I heard screaming coming from the audience, and I could see women trying to stand on their seats—which kept folding up. I asked for the house lights to be brought up to see what was happening. *There was a mouse in the auditorium—running around under the seats!* Can you imagine 400 women with a mouse on the floor? It was pandemonium! What was I to do? Leave the stage? Try to continue? Wait? I returned to the piano, waited a moment, and began to play "Three Blind Mice." I started very slowly, a one-note version that morphed into a lively jazz rendition that had people clapping in time to the music. I finished to a round of applause and everyone was seated again. I divided the audience into groups and led them in a three-part round of "Three Blind Mice" before I resumed my speech. I received a standing ovation at the end of my remarks!

When my party became the majority in the Iowa Legislature, both House and Senate elected new leadership. The House elected enthusiastic, energetic young men who expected to make revolutionary changes immediately, if not sooner. These young men operated under the illusion that since we were all in the same party, everyone would agree with their positions and we could just pass whatever law we wanted. NOT SO. Several weeks later, listening to their frustrated impatience with their colleagues, I burst into song... yes, I really did. Just one single phrase from *The Lion King*. *"I just can't wait to be KING!"* They chuckled sheepishly and they got my point—and we moved on to seek areas of agreement.

A well timed, cleverly delivered moment of humor can have an almost magical effect.

KRISTA SAYS:

Both my grandfathers demonstrated a really fun and thoughtful sense humor. Today, I realize they both made it through significant hardships during some of our country's toughest times. But they retained a love of life and country, a sense of gratitude, and the ability to enjoy life. A big part of this came from not taking themselves too seriously. Grandpa Ross was fond of saying, "Getting up in the morning sure beats the alternative."

I suspect that Mom got a lot of her sense of humor from watching Grandpa Ross. She also learned his ability to approach people in a variety of circumstances and gauge people easily. I refer to this talent as "people reading." And it's Mom's people-reading ability that lets her know her audience and know when to use humor in a given situation.

So what are two helpful hints in using humor to its best advantage?

1. Consider the Source.
2. Know Your Audience.

Keeping these two thoughts in mind has served me well, over and over again. If I attempt to look at an issue or a situation from the perspective of the source, I'm informed enough to know if a laugh or lighthearted response is appropriate or helpful. One example comes from an experience I had when I was new to the commercial real estate leasing business. One of my first really large leases was about to be executed, and the partner of the firm I worked for was a young, successful, good-looking guy who exuded confidence. In the corridor with my immediate boss, who was also a young, successful, good-looking guy, the partner handed the unsigned leases to me and said, "Krista, why don't you put on a fresh coat of lipstick and walk these over and get them signed?" Obviously this was a sexist comment and I would've been fully justified in showing him my displeasure. But I knew his remark was out of character (despite his confidence he was probably nervous about this crucial deal), and I suspected he regretted his blunder as soon as the words left his mouth. So I politely smiled at him, bypassed the lipstick, and took the leases to the new tenant and got them signed.

Without a sense of humor and good people-reading, I could have blown this situation up the wrong way for both me and for him. But knowing my audience I gave him the benefit of the doubt and kept the situation lighthearted. Not taking myself *or* his off-the-cuff blunder too seriously helped me not make a big deal out of his mistake and helped us all remain focused on closing the deal. It extended him forgiveness—even though he probably didn't have the sense to realize in that moment he was lucky to receive it!

Often when I was golfing on vacation with my brother, dad and mom, or sometimes just with my dad, we'd get to the first tee and be waiting our turn to tee off. Sometimes I would play from the same tee as my Dad and my brother. Occasionally a group of guys would begin lamenting how slow it would be playing behind two women. Well, not to worry: We kept our composure, confidently teed up the ball—and then laughed heartily after I bombed my drive down the fairway and saw their jaws hit the grass. Several times the group behind us even applauded and gave me a "nice drive" comment. Relying on a sense of humor in this situation came with a sense of satisfaction for all of us, even for the guys in the foursomes behind us.

The same scenario happened to Scott and me in China when we were paired with two Japanese Airline executives. The looks on their faces were of disappointment and annoyance when we arrived at the first tee—until I hit the ball from the same tees as Scott. Even through the language barrier, their expressions of surprise and then admiration came through crystal clear. Soon enough the expressions were simply of mutual enjoyment of the game we all loved.

So far Mom and I have written about the positive effects of humor, when humor is used to build up. But we all know that there's another side of the coin, when people can use humor to tear down. But in our family, the idea of sarcasm or the style of mean-spirited "gotcha" attempts at humor has never been acceptable. In fact, there've been a few occasions where I had to watch either Mom or Dad refuse to put up with the cynicism of "gotcha" humor.

I recall Dad going through this as President of our country club board. During his tenure of service, the club's executive manager was found to be mismanaging the club's finances. As board President, Dad was ultimately the hiring manager and spokesperson for the decisions made by the board. He had to put up with a lot of cross-fairway barbs, "I told you so's," underhanded comments, and mean-spirited phone calls. But Dad remained "endlessly pleasant" and kept his sense of humor about everything. He knew not to take the criticisms personally, and to know when people were sounding off just because it made them feel better. They didn't care how their behavior made Dad feel, so Dad didn't let himself care in a personal way either. He'd smile, wave, deflect, and go about his own activities with his head held high.

During Mom's political seasons, the "gotcha" attempts were numerous. Opposing party leaders, newspaper and TV reporters, and lobbyists all wanted to try and get in a jab. One year during picture day in the Senate, all the Pages were assembling to have their group photo taken with Mom in "the well" where the Senate President's chair is located. The photographer asked to take an official portrait of Mom first. This was during the Clinton presidency. Mom did not want to have the photo forever in place with President Clinton smiling down on her as the background. So she took it down. When it was time for the Pages' picture, she put it back. One of the Pages made a comment about not wanting President Clinton's portrait photographed in the background behind the Senate President's chair. So they took it down again. Well, this led to a contentious debate, and the Pages got a thorough scolding. Mom took the floor and admitted she "did it first." The story got around, and calls came in from talk show hosts all over the country about the total dust-up over the Iowa Senate President "removing" the President of the United States' portrait from the Senate Chamber. An editorial cartoon appeared on the front page of the local newspaper. The caption under Mom's cartoon image read, "He was leering at us!" This was intended to be a gotcha by the newspaper, but Mom thought it was hilarious and asked the cartoonist to draw the cartoon in watercolor. She has hung it in every office she has occupied since.

Gotcha....or not? Duffy Cartoon 1998

Leading is worlds easier when a sense of humor and a lighthearted style is used effectively, and when your audience, your followers, and the people you'd like to succeed you as leaders understand and respect where you're coming from, and appreciate you. You have to earn this.

A well-timed, well-delivered joke or lighthearted comment can change the entire tenor of a difficult meeting or tense conversation. But it takes guts, practice, a willingness to take some risks, and confidence. By not taking people—including yourself—too seriously, working hard at learning to "read" people, knowing your audience, and taking ownership of humor, negotiation doesn't have to lead to compromise, but to common ground and mutual understanding.

So, take ownership of your humor. Be open to other people's humor. Let humor help you give people the benefit of the doubt. This attitude will serve you well in any arena of life.

For You to Say:

- Can you recall and describe some times when humor has served you well?
- Are there some in your acquaintance who seem to lack a sense of humor? Do you enjoy being in their company?
- Can you describe a time when you might have used humor to defuse a situation?
- Do you recognize cues that let you know humor would be useful and might lead to a better outcome?

Gem Number Eleven: Don't Worry About People Or Things You Cannot Change

It is neither useful nor helpful to worry about who
or what we cannot control.
It's not our job to control or change others.

MARY SAYS:

My mother Geneva was a championship worrier. I often told her that I didn't need to worry because she did enough for both of us. One of her biggest worries was my lack of interest in being a lady. But "well behaved women seldom make history" was my mantra long before I heard it or read it. Somehow, despite being raised by the grand matriarch of worrying, I learned a very important lesson early on: *Worrying about things I could not change (or fix) was a waste of time and energy.*

I hated shopping for clothes in middle school and high school. During most of those years, my clothes were found in the "chubbette" department. Yes, I was fat, and yes, they really called it that! I was embarrassed about being in that category and I hated wearing dresses—and I didn't hesitate to let my mother know how I felt. I can still hear Geneva saying, "Mary, we don't hate, we just strongly dislike." Perhaps those were true words of wisdom, but they did nothing to change my feelings about having to be "ladylike" by wearing dresses. I'll leave the disasters that were our shopping trips to your imaginations.

Mary's "chubbette" Dress Circa 1940's

As I matured, I accepted the fact that my mother could not change. I loved my mother and I wanted a good relationship with her. So I changed. I didn't change my distaste for being "ladylike" or my drive for ambition or my attitude toward wearing dresses. (True confession: Today I have only three dresses in my closet and they are all floor-length formal wear.) What I did change was my conversation and my responses to my mother so that we could enjoy being together. It is a source of great joy for me to remember the lovely relationship I had with Geneva throughout my adult years. Changing the way I shared my feelings with her was a very small price to pay for that.

Ross was a teacher and a coach for many years. He was good at it. Students and parents loved him. When he decided to leave teaching to become one of the pioneer soil conservationists in Iowa, I was too young to understand the risk he took. Men who were breadwinners did not make mid-career risky job changes. *This simply was not done!* In his endlessly pleasant way, he ignored the naysayers and moved on. His desire to preserve the rich black soil in Iowa and his love for the outdoors led him to seek this change. When we were driving along a country road and he saw a farmer fall plowing, he would stop the car, trudge through the field and speak to the farmer about embracing the better conservation practice of low till plowing. Embarrassing for his daughter sitting in the car, but a demonstration of his passion for the work and what he believed in. I am convinced that he remained healthy, active and intellectually curious well into his nineties because he had the courage to pursue his passion. His willingness to pursue opportunity provided a great model for me...it gave me the courage to cast worry aside and take career risks of my own.

Being part of a two-career marriage for fifty-seven years created opportunities for many career decisions, both for Kay and for me. During our second stint in Iowa City, after I received my Master's degree, I became the Assistant Superintendent of Schools. This was *huge!* At the time there were only two other women in Iowa who had achieved that level of administration. I didn't break the glass ceiling, but I bumped my head on it if I stood on my tiptoes.

And then Kay had the opportunity to become the Director of the Midwest Educational Learning Resource Center.

This was a federally funded project that covered an eight-state area, and was charged with helping the states develop media and materials that would allow special needs kids to be mainstreamed into the public school. The opportunity for Kay to make a difference was incredible—of course we were going. But accepting it meant a move to Des Moines, just when it felt like I had reached the pinnacle of success. It felt like my career was over! Many nights after everyone else was asleep I sat on our deck and cried my eyes out. This was a painful "Y" in our road, but my worries over my own career were far secondary: Kay was going to make a huge difference, and staying behind and leaving Kay or the kids never occurred to me. I just needed to feel sorry for myself and whine about it for a while. I did so privately and then I got back to thinking about what I *could* change.

My early efforts to find a job in education in the Des Moines area confirmed my worst fears. No one wanted to hire an outsider, particularly a woman outsider in an administrative position. Too educated, too experienced, too expensive—just not going to happen. My only prospect in education was to return to a classroom. Then a friend introduced me to a headhunter who was seeking candidates for the Director of Personnel for a large retail company. Talk about unqualified—my only retail experience was as a customer.

But, thinking, "What's the worst that can happen?" I went to the interview. And guess what? It was very close to the worst that can happen.

The interview took place in the office of the President of the company, a gorgeous contemporary room. The desk was glass with chrome legs, there was a white shag area rug, white window seats lined one wall, and there were several black and chrome leather chairs surrounding a coffee table. Five men were present. (Later I referred to it as "the gang interview.") They explained how they were on the brink of moving to computerized cash registers and they were fearful that their "very experienced" senior saleswomen could not adapt. Perhaps my educational background could be helpful. It was also the time when Equal Opportunity policies were being implemented by state and federal governments. During this interview I was asked two infuriating questions. The first: "How does your husband feel about you working?" The second: "Who gets dinner at your house?" I answered the first one politely, but the second one got a "None of your business!" response.

I walked out of that interview, called Kay and said I wouldn't work for those *%%$#&^s! (There are times that flouting the Endlessly Pleasant principle is appropriate and called for. This was one of those times.) That was a very quiet evening at our house.

During my final week in Iowa City, the call came: they were offering me the job, and inviting me back for a second interview to discuss the details. Kay and I decided I'd be crazy not to go and listen to the offer.

And it was a great offer—nearly twice the money I had been making in education, and I received an apology for the inappropriate questions. And so I became a Personnel Director. I had an academic background and teaching experience, but no industry knowledge. Both the company and I took a big risk. I was expected to develop a training program to prepare people for a huge change and I had no idea of the substance of the material that should be covered. A big opportunity to fail!

Several thousand people located all around Iowa needed to be trained to use the system when it went live. We trained trainers at each store, and I travelled for a month straight to visit each location. The salespeople welcomed the new system. It was faster and required less handwriting and record keeping. Turns out the "very experienced" senior saleswomen were not only capable of adapting, they loved the new system. Another surprise.

Management, however, was a different story. They were neither interested nor prepared to use the data produced by the new system. They still expected to go out to the floor and rely on the information from the old cash register along with the intuition of the salespeople. A classic example of management saying, "We expect everyone else to change, but we will continue on as we have been. No change for us!"

As it turned out, helping management to see the value of using the data reports in their work was a much larger challenge than teaching the salespeople to use the point of sale computers. Only after senior leaders began using them at meetings did those merchants scramble to learn how to read and interpret those reports.

During my stint in the retail business, a fistfight developed outside the door of the warehouse and carried over into the employee cafeteria. It had racial overtones. One of the participants was brought into my office for discipline. She said I had no right to tell her what to believe. I agreed. Then I fired her. She was furious that I had not fired the other employee. I said, "If she ever shows up again, I will fire her, too."

To the others in the group, I explained that they were entitled to their beliefs and opinions, but they could not share them in the workplace. Any employee who used those words or displayed that type of violent behavior at work would be fired. I did not ask them to change their beliefs; I just explained what behavior was acceptable in the workplace. Setting standards for behavior is appropriate and necessary no matter the setting.

When someone calls or comes to meet with me and is rude—or worse, rude to one of my teammates—I react badly. From time to time in various work settings, I heard very loud, demanding voices outside my door. When that happened I usually got up and made myself visible. Invariably the situation changed, always to a softer volume and more courteous tone. I could not change the fact that the person was rude and obnoxious, but I could change how they behaved in my office. When asked, "Is there a problem here?" the guest would invariably answer "no." I often asked the visitor to take a seat and invited the secretary or receptionist into my office to give their version of the story.

When I heard rudeness or shouting over the phone, I picked up, introduced myself and inquired if there was a problem. Those tactics were immediately effective. My teammate usually received an apology, plus they knew they had my support. My default mode is "endlessly pleasant," but I can and will be very formal and guarded with people who have been rude to my teammates. That formality makes it clear that working with me requires treating me and everyone around me with respect. Education, business, politics, and diplomacy all have their share of difficult people. The task is not to worry about trying to change people, rather to be sure they understand how their actions negatively affect the results they are seeking. It also makes it clear that it is their own behavior that makes it difficult for us to work together. I find it hard to trust someone who demonstrates that kind of "split personality."

As I look back over many diverse career opportunities, I realize that the greatest opportunities came with the biggest risks attached. Every time a new opportunity presented itself, it was because change was urgently needed. The survival of the organization depended on leaders that could embrace change. Willingness to accept and embrace change is a requirement in a career journey. Recognizing the opportunities that change presents, even change that involves risk of negative consequences, is necessary. Each time I have taken a risk, even when I have failed to meet my own expectations, I have learned new skills, understood myself better, and moved ahead in my career journey.

One of the most challenging times of putting aside worry and embracing reasonable risk occurred not in business but in my personal life. When I was working at Wellmark, we undertook a wellness program for all employees. As a part of that effort, we offered free health screens, done on company time, for anyone who wanted them. A health screen provided a baseline of information for each person to make a plan for improving his or her health. Since I was expecting employees to do this I needed to model the behavior, so I was one of the first to participate in the screening.

My results came back with a blood count so low the providers thought they had made a mistake, and asked me to repeat the test. OK, fine. Do it again.

Same result. One of the nurses told me I was so anemic she didn't know how I was remaining upright. Well, I *was* tired, but after all, I was getting older....

More testing followed—and I got a really scary diagnosis. I had colon cancer. Surgery was the only treatment available. We had planned a family trip to Disney World in Florida over Thanksgiving. After speaking with my doctor and the surgeon, we decided to put our very obvious worries about my health aside for this short period of time and go ahead with the trip. We'd schedule the surgery for the Tuesday after our return.

I'm so glad I chose precious family time over worry. That trip remains one of my most cherished memories. At the time we did not know my prognosis—if I was going to be disabled, or dealing with a long recovery, or if I would be facing an imminent threat to my life. But for the duration of the trip we put the worry aside and just enjoyed one another's company in a lovely place. It was such a blessing.

Back in Iowa, I had the surgery and received the best possible news— the surgeon told us she "got it all." I was released from the hospital in three days, and with that kind of good news I healed very quickly. Staff began bringing me work and having meetings at our dining room table within a week of the surgery. It was good to be thinking of something normal—like work!

I had a round of chemotherapy to reduce the risk of reoccurrence. The treatment involved IVs in my hands (usually for about an hour) for five days in a row, once a month for six months. Fortunately I avoided nausea and hair loss and continued serving in the legislature and working with my human resource team. If there was ever a time to be thankful for good teams, that was it. My team at the Legislature and my team at Wellmark held me up for six months.

Meanwhile at home Kay was my rock, encouraging me to keep going, and pulling me back when I went too far too fast. Later he volunteered as a Board member with the Cancer Society and served for many years. For several of those years, he owned a limousine and picked up people at nursing homes and hospitals for doctor's appointments or other cancer treatments. He wore a chauffeur's cap and people looked forward to him coming to drive them.

Kay and his 'Road to Recovery' Limo Circa 1990's

As of today I've been cancer-free for almost 15 years. I am a cancer survivor—in large part because of the invaluable support systems I had and continue to have.

KRISTA SAYS:

My learnings about the "art of worry" can go in many directions. First, I may have inherited the champion worrier gene from my Grandma Geneva—but with a different application. My particular struggle with worry was about feeling judged by others and seeking my own version of the Good Housekeeping Seal of Approval. At one time peer pressure was huge. WWPT (What Will People Think) was paramount. Worry about pleasing my parents, my grandparents, my brother, my friends, my teachers, my employers . . . and the list goes on.

By my college years, I had perfected the "art of worry" into debilitating test anxiety and wanting desperately to excel in school. Translate this "worry" into the demands I placed on myself to be the perfect student, the perfect sorority girl, the woman who would graduate with high honors like her brother did, who would leave college with the perfect life planned out in front of her.

Translate again into fear of the unknown. I had no real plan. I think I was comfortable coasting along, "sort of" figuring it out for the short term. I was an expert at generalizing internally. I thought I was the only person in the world who ever struggled with tests, with speaking up for myself, with wanting to do well in everything. (I hadn't yet learned the Mastery is Optional principle!)

Under pressure to play well on the golf course, my inability to deal with fear and worry as a mental part of my game management meant that my anxieties too often triumphed over my physical skills and talents as a player. It was my roadblock in attempting to pass the PGA playing ability test after trying so many times.

I didn't come to this realization until years and years later, but I believe I was looking outside myself for approval and acceptance, evaluating everything I was doing according to external parameters. Let me emphasize that no one in my family ever demanded, suggested, or even mentioned the expectations by which I was judging myself. No, I created those yardsticks all on my own, and I judged myself against the successes of my mother, my father, and my brother. I wanted to live up to or even exceed their accomplishments. Getting the perfect grade or achieving the target score in golf were examples of greatness, and I was not satisfied with the results that my endless comparing revealed. But in living by a measuring stick that compared me to someone else's results, I deprived myself of developing my *own* measures of success for years. In fact it's still a challenge that creeps into my head from time to time when I allow it.

For me, "Don't worry about what you can't control" was something I had to learn. I had to teach it to myself and practice it, and I still have to work on it. Don't you? I'm sure you know people who need to practice this. If we had the power of mind reading or clairvoyance would we be free from worry? Maybe so. However, we are not wired that way. This is a huge point. A satisfying life requires us to accept, to have faith in ourselves and in the unknown, and in the higher powers we believe in.

This means I will not be the mirror copy of my mother, my father, my brother, some golfer, or another person I admire. It means I accept that I am unique—one of a kind—and I celebrate it! All the neat qualities and attributes about how I am wired make up my frame of reference and experiences—and I've learned that I can take the very things that make me different from everyone else and use them to my benefit and for the benefit of others. It took me until I was 40-something to get this. What's important is I *do* get it and I have a positive message about it.

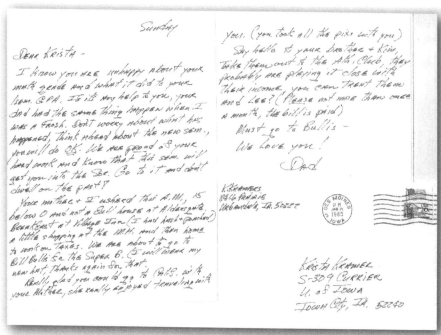

Note from Kay to Krista After First Semester
Grades Received at U. of Iowa 1985

After reading how Mary learned to manage her relationship with Geneva, you probably have a clue that she approached her role as a mother differently than her upbringing. Yes, there has always been the foundation of Christian values, a core of integrity and the necessity of treating people with respect. Yet I look back and see so many places where listening, hearing, asking, and sorting through things with my parents helped me address my worrying habit, because I was not expected to fit in any mold.

Still, I wrestled with a fear of the unknown. I was trapped in my fear of making bad choices, bad judgments and worrying about making any choice that would be wrong for me. And trust me, I've made some questionable choices and judgments. (As I write this, picture me shaking my head, smiling, just being thankful for surviving a couple of those choices!)

But slowly over time, I learned to apply Mom's question to situations: "What's the worst that can happen?" When I began to consider things from that perspective, my fears about poor choices, judgment and worry began to diminish significantly. It is this meaningful frame of reference from my own growth and journey that provides great support in the coaching work I now do. Now I'm asking: "What's the *best* that can happen?"

We live in a culture where we allow ourselves to believe we have control over so much. Well guess what? We don't. Accepting that we don't control very much, we can learn to accept change, even chaos. By accepting what we cannot control, we liberate each of our spirits to focus on those things we *can* control and improve.

Among my professional experiences, one (thankfully short) chapter in which an employer attempted to control me stands out. I worried about the way he was treating me, and I wanted him to change his behavior. Meanwhile *he* expected me to change *my* behavior! Neither of us was going to give on this one; we were simply operating on two different playing fields. He was more academic, regulatory and institutional; I was more relational, flexible and negotiable. Our clients preferred my style and asked to work with me. I didn't sense any sort of respect coming my way, yet he demanded I respect him. I had to learn to distinguish when a person's rejection of me (real or perceived) is not an action toward me that I should take personally. It was more about him than about me. It was a short chapter in my career journey, no more than 5-6 months, but at the time it was excruciating.

Finally I decided to worry about what I *could* change—and it wasn't going to be my boss. So in an act of self-preservation, I resigned from the job before I was set up for more anguish and possibly eventual termination. Resigning was one of the best professional decisions I have ever made, even though I did not have another job lined up. Yes, it involved risk, but I left with respect for myself, and it resulted in fueling my entrepreneurial spirit!

Remember, the only thing you control is the ability to adapt and to change yourself. Be prepared to embrace change when it represents opportunity. Change may cause discomfort, but almost always leads to opportunity.

For You to Say:

- Describe your single biggest worry, whether it's personal or professional. Is it in your control? If not, how can you change the way you think about it and react to it?
- What's your first reaction to something that requires you to change?
- How do you react to someone or something you can't change? Do you worry about it? Do you keep considering alternatives? Can you move on to a more productive place?
- Do you have a method of recognizing what you can control and what you cannot control?

Gem Number Twelve: Manage Your Time. It Does Not Manage You.

Surprise yourself! You have a lot more time than you think—but only if you PRIORITIZE.

MARY SAYS:

Managing time is the second-most important skill for a musician. It comes right behind "perfect practice makes perfect." Beginning in middle school, there were many hours of rehearsal with groups, and more hours of practice for lessons. If I wanted to participate in other activities like team sports, I had to be present at practices and games. When to do the homework? I never wanted to miss anything, so my balancing act began early.

In high school, I had the marvelous experience of becoming a member of the University of Iowa Symphony Orchestra. Rehearsals took place every Tuesday and Thursday evening for two hours. If there was a concert upcoming, we practiced Friday evening as well, with the performances on the weekends. Time available for lessons and homework still had to be found, and I wanted to continue playing on the mixed volleyball and women's basketball teams. This meant more practices and more games. There weren't enough hours...so I had to make them all count.

Then I began playing the organ for church services, weddings and funerals as well as accompanying a variety of individuals and groups. I was happy to make the time because I was getting paid. Time became even more precious.

I complained about needing more time until someone shared this idea. You're exhausted, finally lay your head on the pillow at night, give a big sigh and close your eyes. Suddenly a voice says, "Get up! You can have two more hours today." Would that be a good thing? My answer is still an emphatic NO. We all are given the same amount of time...it's how we choose to use it that matters.

When I was first elected to the Iowa Legislature, my Party was in the minority and it was entirely possible for me to maintain my full-time job at the insurance company and serve effectively in the Legislature. Yes, it meant sixty-hour weeks reading bills and returning office emails until the wee hours, but I had lived that kind of schedule most of my life. However, when my Party took the majority of the Iowa Senate and I was elected the President of the Senate, things changed. I was expected to preside over debate, and manage the back of the chamber processes as well. It didn't take long to realize I had two full-time jobs.

What to do? Kay and I agreed something must go and we decided I should retire from the insurance company. Not the best *financial* decision for us, but one that made the most sense if I wanted to continue my public service. I scheduled a meeting to discuss my retirement plans with my boss, the CEO. During our discussion he offered another alternative. I could leave my position as Vice President of Human Resources, and become Director of the company Foundation. His vision of the desired future involved a new focus for the Foundation. This would involve working with communities, and providing grants to projects that would improve population-wide health. I really wanted to help accomplish that vision. Here was another great opportunity to make a difference. I still had two full-time jobs, but they both had enough flexibility that I could accomplish the important things of both with the help of my teammates. Sometimes we have to give ourselves permission to say "I can't continue to have all this on my plate and do the job that needs to be done." Accepting this reality is not failure! Sometimes we need to give ourselves permission to decide what matters enough to continue doing and what we can stop.

This principle applies to family or personal matters as much as career. Who was that crazy woman racing on the interstate with store-bought cupcakes in the back seat? Me, trying to get the birthday cupcakes to Krista's 4th grade class at the promised time! There was a long list of stuff to do at the office but delivering those cupcakes was both urgent and important, and the to-do list was still there after dinner that night and the next morning. Celebrating a birthday with her classmates was a once-a-year celebration for Krista. I have written about how much I love to cook, and making treats was always fun for me. But that year my schedule simply did not include time for baking cupcakes, so I made a stop at the bakery...without an ounce of guilt that I hadn't made them myself. Neither Krista nor her classmates cared whether they were homemade or not.

During my years in human resources, I had many learning opportunities. One that has served me well is the Steven Covey Time Management Program "First Things First." It is a very simple system for approaching the many "to-dos" of life. I'll share just a summary here. Keep in mind that *you* decide what is urgent and what is important. Too many times we let other people's urgency take over!

Practicing the principle of First Things First can be life-changing. Divide your time into four quadrants using these categories:

Urgent and important;
Urgent, but not important;
Important, but not urgent;
Neither urgent nor important.

Instead of making your "to-do" list, use this table and place each action needed in the proper box. Then you can easily focus on the activities in the box Urgent AND Important. *Always put the urgent and important first.*

Urgent and Important	Urgent, but Not Important
Important, but Not Urgent	**Neither Urgent Nor Important**

This system has been very effective for me. Krista has another system that is very effective for her...choose what works for you!

Finally, over the years of working at managing my time, the Serenity Prayer has served me well. It says: "God give me the serenity to accept the things I cannot change, the courage to change the things I can, and the wisdom to know the difference." Those words have helped me to accept, to have courage, and on my best days, to act with wisdom.

KRISTA SAYS:

Rather than thinking about managing time, I prefer a concept I call Manage Me. We all wake up every day with the same amount of hours, minutes and seconds available. It is up to us to take ownership of time and to manage it according to our own needs and desires.

Manage Me includes managing my emotions as they relate to getting stuff done (or not done). It includes managing my Yesses and my Nos. Manage Me includes deciding whom I agree to work with, do things for, or accept roles for as a volunteer or leader or both. Management guru Peter Drucker observed, "Most of us will have to learn to manage ourselves. We have to learn to develop ourselves. We will have to place ourselves where we can make the greatest contributions. And we will have to stay mentally alert and engaged during a 50-year working life, which means knowing how and when to change the work we do." I have learned how and when to change *Me Management*, how I allocate and spend my time.

Back in high school, golf was an important teacher of Me Management, though I didn't realize it at the time. Mother Nature only provided so much daylight, and practice sessions had to be dedicated to developing skills that could make the biggest impacts for lower competitive scores. As a team we'd get to the course or practice areas as quickly as we could after school, knowing we would work on as much as we could while the daylight lasted. We'd get a good idea of how much time we allocated to repetitious hitting, putting, and grass short game vs. days when we'd play nine holes as practice rounds.

Now back then, I chose not to spend my time practicing from the bunker. I had a block where the sand play was concerned. Because I didn't like it, I avoided practicing getting out of it. Had I dedicated more of my time to bunker practice on a regular basis, it wouldn't have taken me until I was age 34 and in Arizona getting short game lessons at a golf school to "get over" the threat of bunker play and understand how vital making the choice to use my time to practice bunker shots would have benefitted me and my scores.

Another important change in my Me Management occurred when I was transitioning from college to the real world. I was a master procrastinator, and I'm still a bit of an adrenaline junkie. I waited till the last minute to meet deadlines, and then used all my hours, minutes, and seconds up to the very deadline! And for better or for worse, I became good at it. This was how I managed me in the college setting.

Obviously, this management style wasn't going to work with any level of effectiveness in a professional setting. My first job out of college was at a country club. During business hours, members and staff made requests and demands of me and my department that had to be handled, managed, and taken care of—*promptly*, no questions asked. If you ever have challenges with your time managing or your Me Managing, spend a season of your life in a relationship-driven, customer-focused role. When your performance is measured by the resulting satisfaction of those you provide service to, you will either quickly step up and manage yourself more effectively, or you will not remain in a customer-focused role for very long. A realistic sense of urgency takes practice. Somewhat like a hospital triage, you must quickly discern what's first, second, third, and what can wait until after lunch or tomorrow. Not exactly the four quadrants of Mr. Covey, but a functional system!

Customer-focused environments like clubs, specialty stores and your own shop or business are ideal places to master the art of Me Management. If you do not manage your choices related to your time effectively, your livelihood will reflect it. I suppose it's fair to say that nearly all of the professional roles I've chosen and pursued throughout my career are customer- or people-focused. My love of feeling good about my contributions, enjoying praise and positive recognition, and building my own independent praise and recognition system attracts me to the people-focused spaces. I have worked hard to be a master of "good timing." There's a nice adrenaline rush associated with this.

Friends and family often laugh about the tendency Mom and I both have to be "on the way." (I'm grateful that these offenses are lovingly tolerated by those closest to us.) My friend Patty says that for many of our younger years, I operated on California time, while she operated on Central time. Being the master multi-tasker and adrenaline junkie, the more stuff I had to do, the more efficient I was in accomplishing things. Yet the minute I "unplugged" or switched gears into my personal down time, I would fall into an attitude of "what's the hurry?" My sense of urgency lapsed, which really is annoying to the people I love and enjoy being around. By working hard to make a conscious shift toward honoring a time or deadline I'd committed to and developing a greater respect for my friends' and family members' time (not just selfishly my time), I am now operating in the same time zone with those closest to me. I have had a few relapses here and there, but each one teaches me more and more about managing me.

As a business owner, essentially a one-woman operation, Me Management is consistently important. And the more I work with my clients to help them develop better "me managing" habits and calendaring skills, the better I become. There are many tools to select from to effectively manage one's time. My most successful illustration has developed out of the idea of a **Life & Time Menu.** This information is intertwined between years of Franklin Covey's "What Matters Most and Focus" practice, my journey into Coaching, and my own personal foundation and development work.

Each person shows up to work with me with his or her own vision, goals, life details and purposes. And even if they do not, I'm prepared to help them start there. We begin with these questions:

- How would you visualize your Life & Time Menu?
- What would you include on the menu?

Just as a lunch menu might list Starters, Salads, Sandwiches, Big Plates, and Desserts that would let us create the unique meal that suits our desires and dietary considerations, our Life & Time Menu allows us to organize our goals and create a unique "meal" based upon our personal and professional goals. What do you want to "order" for the day? **The Life & Time Menu helps you choose wisely.**

To show you an example, let's work with my Life & Time Menu. The sections on my Menu, which I'll explain in turn, are:

KK'S LIFE & TIME MENU

KK Time
Business Goals
Self-Matters
The Best
Stuff to Accept / Live With

KK Time is the list of activities that bring me personal enjoyment and fulfillment. So my menu choices under KK Time are:

- Personal phone calls
- Personal correspondence
- Daily Delights (making my latte/drinking a smoothie/reading)
- Personal Facebook updating
- Meal planning
- Orderliness (tidying my home/office)
- Walking my dog, Guinness
- Winemaking study

In my Business Goals section, my menu choices are:

- Relationship maintenance
- Client communication

- Business development/marketing
- Blogging/Updating my website
- Networking
- Day to day accounting and operational details
- Reading to stay current with Coaching and Consulting best practices as well as popular thought leaders.

My other categories are Self-Matters (or Self-Care), The Best (time with my hub/family), and finally Stuff to Accept/Live With (like drive time to get to and from a meeting, or any of the other unavoidables in my life that I accept). The "Stuff" menu item can be excessive and add up quickly. In fact, I challenge you to make notes about examples of your Stuff—interruptions, time wasters, "little fires" that may come up and need to be "put out" from time to time.

When you sit down to plan out your own Life & Time Menu, it's helpful to have a clear vision of your personal and professional goals in mind. But even if you don't, the Life & Time Menu can help you visualize those goals—and then organize your day around making them happen. Another thing to keep in mind is that your menu choices don't have to happen at the same time every day, or on the same day each week. The idea of the Menu allows for *flexibility*, yet it is also *intentional, specific and purposeful* because it represents each individual's choices for how he or she dedicates their time.

Once you do have your Menu planned, it's time to strategize about how to make those goals happen. What tools are you using to keep track of your time and schedule? I manage my daily tasks and appointments with my Google cloud-based calendar. This calendar syncs to my iPhone and iPad, so it's with me on all my devices or simply at my desktop. I use an Excel spreadsheet to keep a model of the Menu sections and choices. As with any restaurant, the menu changes from time to time, perhaps seasonally, or otherwise. For example, when I have served a term on a committee or fulfilled a "term of office" on a volunteer board, I update the spreadsheet. I try to make a point of reviewing this every quarter. (Some years in my world operate from January 1 to December 31, and some operate from July 1 to June 30.) But as I'm a kinesthetic learner, I also employ handwritten lists. The physical act of writing things down and crossing items off of a to-do list works well for me. Usually these are short. Often these are my "awake in the middle of the night, write it down to quiet my mind" lists. A lot of these details end up in my calendar as a task with a reminder.

But your tools may be different. If you don't yet have a system in place, I'd encourage you to think about and give meaningful consideration to how you best function and best learn. Are you a tactile or kinesthetic learner? If so you may want to use a handwritten Life & Time Menu. Or maybe you're a visual learner. If so, a Menu with backgrounds, shapes, and color-coded menu items may work best for you. If you're an auditory learner, maybe programming your smartphone or computer to prompt you with audible reminders can keep you on task.

Because a Life & Time Menu is customized to *your* personal preferences and *your* personal goals and activities, you can organize it any way you want. Some of my clients love vertical lists like Excel spreadsheets. Some prefer a lined diary calendar. Some decorate their Life & Time Menus with doodles and scribbles, and still others are strictly digital, with their Life & Time Menu stored on the cloud and synced with their work and home calendars.

One of the beauties of the Life & Time Menu concept is that it can fit into any tool you want it to. Again, it's a unique choice, and we all endeavor to make the right choices about the tools we use to track our time and prepare and modify our schedules.

Now let's look at an issue that nearly always comes up when people are preparing their Life & Time Menus: balancing self-care time and their regular scheduling requirements. Sometimes it's easy to get to a place where we might ask, "How is there enough space for both self-care and schedule?" When it comes to a choice between the two, think for a moment, "How often do we make the choice in favor of The Schedule versus Self-Care?"

Roger Browner, an author who writes about leadership and executive successes wrote, "When you schedule every minute of your workday you don't have time to put out the small fires that come up all day long. Solution: only schedule 40-50 percent of your day." The first step to getting organized may be to take a long look at **who** is doing the scheduling and **how** it is being done.

Although most of us busy people tend to feel overextended and that too many demands are being made upon us, most of us do not stop to recognize that *we have more control over our time than we think we do.*

Somewhere along the line we came to believe that success would be achieved when we had every minute scheduled. We have come to equate full schedules to full productivity. Yet Roger Browner, having interviewed the most successful CEOs and top business leaders, tells us that they have learned to schedule only 40-50% of their working day. What a concept! If it works for them, it might be worth trying.

Again, it's about choices! I'd like to suggest three additions to Browner's remarks:

1. Try not to anticipate that just because we don't plan every moment that those little fires will *necessarily* arrive. Instead, consider that 40-50% window as open space or spaciousness within your life. A good friend once shared that she likes to leave open spaces to allow for the universe to send in the good stuff. If she's not open, that good stuff has no room to come in. This is the perfect time for self-care to be a part of "the schedule." You'll be more authentic, focused, unhurried, and fully present. That's a nice gift to give yourself and everyone around you.

2. Think of how to realistically allocate for how much time you do need to plan for your Menu details. And remain in touch with reality versus optimism as you plan. My tendency is a default positive hope that I can do more than I give myself time for. Marshall Goldsmith referred to this as "wading into the sea of optimism." I often wade in farther than I can realistically swim. So I've learned to shift my thinking to realistic planning from optimistic planning. This takes practice!

3. "No" is a complete sentence. So if there isn't room for any more in your schedule or calendar, don't bring anything else in there.

We're all good at holding/creating space for others to assist them in being the best they can be. So in the area of scheduling and time planning, we need to build in time for self-care so we are assisting ourselves in being the best we can be, too. If this is a particular challenge for you, consider engaging an accountability partner to journey with you. Document your commitments to yourself right there in your Life & Time Menu, just as you would document a commitment to a vision, mission, dream or goal. Your signature alongside your written commitment to employ consistency in your LIFE is significant.

By spending time with your Life & Time Menu each week, you're giving yourself permission to be consistent and committed on a higher level to YOUR time and YOUR schedule. "Manage Your Time, It Does Not Manage You." Why? **Time does not manage you; your choices manage time.**

For You to Say:

- Try placing and prioritizing your tasks into the four quadrants. Making decisions about the placement of your activities will give you insight into how you make calendar commitments. Review your calendar commitments by the four quadrants for a month to determine if you are focusing on those things that are both urgent and important.
- Can you learn to ignore those things others want you to label urgent until you have decided what is both urgent and important to you?
- Can you choose one or two things in the "neither urgent nor important" box and give yourself permission just to enjoy them?
- Do you allow yourself to save some time to read something for pleasure, to exercise, to take a long walk, or just to sit and think?
- Being intentional about time management is a necessary part of determining where you are today. Analyze your calendar

for the last month to compare how your calendar commitments match up with the things you say you value most. Are you giving time to the right stuff?

- Describe for yourself those things you must do—earn a living, support yourself and others who depend on you, etc. Then be realistic about what else you can take on.
- Do you need to prioritize or postpone some things?
- You have decades to accomplish things—but some of the important stuff has time limits. Parenting, for example. The kids grow up! Give yourself permission to realistically decide what things you have time to do now beyond those things you know you must do. What can you delay or postpone?

Gem Number Thirteen: Skills Create Opportunities

Inventory your skill set.
Not satisfied? Then learn something new:
Take a class, get a coach, ask for advice, choose a
mentor.
RAISE YOUR HAND!

MARY SAYS:

The opportunity to study with University-level music professors as a high school sophomore was huge and provided me opportunities for performance experience far beyond anything I had ever dreamed. But the opportunity came with huge risks and difficult circumstances. The Thursday afternoon seminar required every student to perform at least four times a semester. Many of these students were in graduate school and had performed all over the country. To meet expectations (not to mention justify my presence in the class) I had to perform at their level. The critiques were harsh and at the time seemed merciless. I learned quickly to listen without defending myself, then to get out of the room before crying. Crying would have been unforgivable in that setting.

Two things happened as a result of this experience. First, I determined I was not in the same league as my classmates. But I determined I would get better—I could and *would* perform at their level.

To achieve that level there was only one thing to do: practice, practice, practice. By putting in countless hours and working that hard, I achieved the goal of playing at least as well as my peers. My motivation was not so much for me to play well as it was to compete—to play as well as my peers in that class. There would always be students who were more gifted than I, but I could hold my own. Second, I determined no one would ever see my nerves or my fear! The risk-reward equation was perfectly clear. As it turned out hiding fear and nerves is a requirement for public speaking, which came along a lot later in my life.

When I began my position in the retail company, I had an academic background and teaching experience, but no knowledge of the industry. What I knew about retailing was learned as a customer. As it turned out, the customer perspective was the most important. The company and I took a very big risk. I had the skills to develop curriculum and teach it, but the content in this case was completely foreign to me. There was no pattern in place for the changes I was expected to make. In other words, I was facing a huge opportunity to fail.

My ability to train employees, develop curriculum, help people to accept change and adapt to new systems led to the call from the headhunter that ultimately led me to the insurance business. A total business system had been installed and it nearly brought the company to its knees. After it was announced that I had accepted a position at the insurance company, several of my friends told me confidentially, "You don't want to go there, it's a terrible place to work." Perhaps, but it was also an opportunity to become an officer of a major company—a position few other women in Iowa held at that time. I went.

And it *was* a terrible place to work! Fortunately for me I had the power to make changes and I believed I could succeed. Early in my time there, the CEO of the company expressed concern about me encouraging employees to call me by my first name. My position was that this level of familiarity was necessary to make myself approachable. Because of completely new business processes, employees were being asked to change almost everything about their workplace and their jobs. They needed to believe that someone in top management was paying attention to them and was available to them. So I told the CEO I thought it was best that I was viewed as an approachable advocate for employees. He responded, "But they need to respect you, you're an officer of this company. Just like they need to respect me. I'm the CEO, the Captain of the ship." My answer? "Yes sir, you are the Captain of this ship. But right now, your rudder isn't attached to anything!"

It took over a year to get that rudder attached to a productive company culture.

Some years later, on a Saturday morning, three women rang the doorbell, unannounced. When Kay answered the door, one of them said to him, "You are *going* to support this!"

"Ah, hello…" said a startled Kay, and then let me know I had visitors.

These women had come to invite me to run for the Iowa Senate. I said no. At the time I was working over sixty hours a week.

But a former Governor of Iowa was my boss, and they planned to visit with him about it next. I decided that if anyone was going to visit with my boss, I should go with them. So we all trooped over to his house . . . and he graciously and patiently explained the pros and cons of running for office and then serving in the legislature. He emphasized the importance of a part-time legislature—and I really agreed with that! But then he said the most important thing: "The company will support you if you decide to do this." So I said I would consider it.

Back at home I discussed the possibility with Kay. I knew I had the skill to serve, but I was clueless about campaigning. The next two weeks involved gathering signatures for my nomination papers. I delivered my signed petitions to the Secretary of State's Office—and I was on the ballot.

Fortunately for me, the women who recruited me promised to stay with me—and they did. I got the graduate course in how to campaign over the weekend after I turned in my nomination papers. And then it was knocking on doors every afternoon from 4 PM till dark. Then going home and making phone calls to ask for money to support the campaign. Signs were designed and printed (I dislike yard signs to this day!). Media was discussed—ads and print designs and decisions were completed and time and space was purchased. Forums were scheduled—I needed to get in front of every audience I could. On election eve, I threw away five pairs of shoes I had completely worn out while door knocking the neighborhoods. But it all paid off! I won.

After the first four years in the Senate my party became the majority and I was elected the President of the Senate. This was a great honor to be sure, to know that my colleagues thought I could preside over debate in the Senate Chamber. What I did not know at the time was the job of President also required managing the processes and the people who wrote the bills, did the research, and cleaned and maintained the legislative chambers. Who knew? Fortunately I had some leadership experience and I knew something about the processes so I hired an "A" team, including a new Secretary of the Senate...and together we got the job done. I had been given the gavel. It was up to me to use it.

When the call came from the White House inviting me to consider serving as a U.S. Ambassador to Barbados and the Eastern Caribbean, I had no idea where the country was, let alone what an Ambassador was supposed to accomplish. But when the President of the United States calls to say, "Mary, we need some of that Iowa common sense down there," the correct answer is, "Yes Sir, we accept." I had virtually no background knowledge, but I knew I could surmount a steep learning curve and that my previous skills could be used to serve. And I was right about that—the Ambassador role *did* allow me to use every skill I had developed throughout my life. From music, to education, to business, to politics . . . every bit of learning was applicable. The learning curve was formidable, and I felt more pressure to achieve than at any other time in my life. My new boss was the President of the United States! But by that time I had many life experiences to rely on, a robust set of skills, and the wisdom to seek help from the most knowledgeable sources when I needed it. Again I assembled an A team, and we got some real work done.

It is not only about skills, it is about the confidence that says *I may not know it now—but I can learn*. And then admit you don't know everything, seek out people who do know and are willing to teach you and share their knowledge with you. Sometimes the learning is like drinking from the fire hose, but it is not necessary to retain everything everyone thinks is important....You will know what you need to know!

Mary Sworn in as U.S. Ambassador by Secretary of State Colin Powell 2004

KRISTA SAYS:

In Mom's case, it's safe to say that opportunities found her. Even when she was faced with leaving Iowa City in the late 70's and finding a new career in Des Moines (the move that left her crying secretly on the deck, if you'll remember), it truly was an opportunity in disguise.

Now in my case, *opportunity seeker* is a good description for me. Because I live in the "Mastery is Optional" world, one might look over my life (career chapters especially) and make the observation that I am driven by a need to continually learn new skills and develop new talents. I dream of and foresee innovation…new, different ways of succeeding in the professional arena or in helping people. I enjoy, and even thrive on, change and risk. Have I learned some difficult, but valuable lessons with this attitude? Absolutely.

When you are a quick study, with a demonstrated track record of attacking new things and succeeding quickly, you are often given the opportunity to do more—along with the request to do it faster and faster. This presents wonderful opportunities . . . until you find you are taking on too much. Your satisfaction levels may decrease and burnout becomes a real problem, or, as was the case in one of my work-world examples, the compensation just didn't keep up with the responsibilities.

More than once, I found myself at a crossroads: I was enjoying and thriving on lots of responsibility, but the rewards weren't there. (A couple of my employers missed the memo about Positive Recognition and Modeling the Way.) These "crossroads moments" led me to further opportunity seeking—new job searches, and often a total change in course professionally. Thankfully, I was able to transition my skills effectively in every new position. When you know your skills and your strengths and can confidently discuss them, you can create opportunities.

The very first career opportunity I wanted—working at the golf shop—my Dad helped me get my foot in the door. But it was up to me to "seal the deal," and by enthusiastically describing the internship program to my future boss and describing how and why my previous retail training, experience and skills would benefit the golf shop, I won him over and got the job.

Now, what if you're in a situation in which opportunity doesn't knock?

In many career tracks, we find ourselves waiting to be promoted, often far longer than we want to. The person ahead of us in line must be promoted or must leave in order for our promotion to come along. There's a time and place for patience (see the Practice

Patience Gem!), but not if it means sitting passively by for extended periods of time and leaving the outcome of your career and dreams in other people's hands. During my real estate career I sought opportunities to take on more responsibility, to earn more, and to prove to myself I could do more. With the exception of the times I was self-employed, as I am now, I have changed jobs through my own opportunity-seeking every two or three years. This way I am constantly learning new things and continually growing my skill set.

I have high expectations of myself, and admittedly, can often be too hard on myself. When you grow up watching the three other members of your immediate family excel and enjoy their achievements, you want to taste it and enjoy achievement, too. To me it's kind of like caffeine: I look forward to achieving; I crave it. It feels good to look in the mirror and acknowledge my accomplishments. But in classic overachiever mode, that sense of accomplishment is followed by "What's next?"

Over time, the "What's next?" challenges I've sought or created for myself have grown larger and tougher. I invest more and more of myself and my time and hard work in learning, growing, developing and striving to "get there."

I am the person who doesn't hear "No." I am the person who looks for the "workaround," the person who, in the face of a challenge, says, "We can find a way to do this." It's a skill I love to celebrate.

In my volunteer roles, I seek opportunities in the same way. When I joined my local Rotary Club in 2010, part of our leadership succession plan had some gaps. Two years after I joined, when there was still no appointed successor to the current President, I saw an opportunity. I looked into the rules for how one works his or her way into the office of Club President, and, finding no specific requirements, simply asked for the opportunity. The Club gave it to me, and I threw myself into the role. During my year of service as President, our membership grew by 54% and our member participation in service projects increased. Our engagement with our District increased, and the energy at our weekly meetings was vibrant and thriving. The day I concluded my service term, I had a major achievement rush—euphoric, really. And I'm proud I asked for that opportunity because two years later I have even more improved leadership skills and opportunities in Rotary, and other organizations are seeking me. What an awesome feeling!

Krista Rotary Speaker 2014

Now let's move from the professional arena to the personal. What are you really, really good at? One of my earliest skills was golf. What's yours? Is it tennis? Art? Photography? Dance? A musical instrument like piano or guitar? What is it?

I'm asking you to identify it because it is a huge confidence builder. And, I want you to seek opportunities to show it off. When your professional or volunteer colleagues become your audience and observe you demonstrating skills you love and at which you excel, your stock goes up. If you have significant competence in a certain area, it shows your discipline and dedication to a craft, whether it's an athletic skill or a musical or art-related talent. This shows how capable you are in developing in other roles within your professional or volunteer endeavors. Do not be shy about sharing these skills.

When word got out among my commercial real estate peers that I had "game," my stock went up. It was my opportunity to "play from the men's tees" in many instances. In the mid 90's real estate was a male-dominated field, and there were only a handful of women in commercial real estate in Chicago who had the skills, knowledge and mental toughness to accept an invitation to play golf with the executives, clients, and building owners with whom we frequently did business. I was often one of the better players in a foursome. What did I gain as a result of these experiences and demonstrating these skills? I had an audience to see me engaged outside of the usual space where people would see me. My self-confidence came out more, and the ability to "dig deep" under pressure truly helped my employers and executives appreciate my potential as a team member and "player" in the commercial real estate space.

The name for the company I own and operate today came about as a result of my golf skills. There was a group of 15-20 women who worked in some capacity in the commercial real estate space who were really interested in improving their golf skills and knowledge. They formed a social group called Chicks with Sticks and asked me to get involved. The concept was to provide basic playing skills help, a rules and etiquette overview, and a forum to answer questions. From this relationship, the idea of She Kan! Golf was born.

Later when I became an independent contractor for a residential real estate company, I created She Kan! Kompany in the spirit of She Kan! Golf. I have been operating She Kan! Kompany since 2002 and it has now evolved from to KK Hartman Coaching LLC dba She Kan! Kompany to KK Hartman Partners, LLC. I'm proud of it. My one-woman business still provides a forum to answer (and now to ask) powerful questions. Transitioning from "basic playing skills for golf," I now work in the space of life skills improvement with all my clients. And we work far beyond the basics. Each professional has his or her own set of rules and etiquette to abide by within a profession's culture, and we work together to the relationship and business development skills that will help each client succeed.

Remember, skills do create opportunities. Do not be afraid to take a risk in seeking opportunities.

For You to Say:

- What is your best skill? What do you love to do?
- Are there skills you could pursue that would get you closer to your vision of the desired future?
- Do you remember a time you raised your hand and got great results?

- Is there a time you did not raise your hand and now regret not going for it?
- How will you approach opportunities in the future?
- Imagine one or two opportunities you could seek right now.

Gem Number Fourteen: When Opportunity Knocks...or Not

When opportunity knocks...will you open the door?
So it's not knocking—take action!

MARY SAYS:

Opportunity comes in many sizes and flavors. Try not to say yes or no immediately. Before you make a decision, determine the risk factors. Ask yourself these four questions.

1) Do I want to do this?

That is the first and most important question. Is this something I really want to do? Do I have a passion for doing this? Am I seeking this change because I need to get away from the current situation? Do I have the skills or can I learn the skills necessary to do it. Can I balance the other parts of my life if I say yes?

2) Can I maintain my values and my integrity if I do this?

What tradeoffs will be expected? Is the group or the company honest? Are they doing something worthwhile? Will I be proud to talk about my membership in this group?

This question was hardest for me when I was considering entering politics. I finally decided I could maintain my integrity and represent my constituents fairly. And the best happened.

3) If I take the risk what's the worst that can happen?

If the answer to this is "I might fail," do not accept that as a good enough reason to stop considering the opportunity. Have enough confidence in your ability to learn and to manage so that if you fail you are able to move forward and make another change.

4) If I take the risk what's the best that can happen?

I may succeed beyond my wildest dreams. I may find the stepping stone to my next big dream. I might make a big difference in the lives of the people around me. I might change something in my community for the better.

So, your answers to questions one and two are yes. And questions three and four have you believing you are ready to make a leap. What next?

Before you make the call or the appointment to say yes, have a plan for saying yes. Prepare yourself for the process of change. Will you move? Who will take your place? Have you accounted for financial issues and changes to insurance? Who needs to know what you are going to do and in what order? Avoid hurt feelings by saying goodbye before the news is widely known. Prepare yourself to receive congratulations graciously. Prepare yourself to have people ask, "What are you doing? Are you sure about this?"

There will be hard things to face...but great things await. GO FOR IT!

KRISTA SAYS:
As I mentioned when we talked about "Skills Creating Opportunities," what if opportunity doesn't knock? How and where will you find opportunity? A great place to start is to review your vision and goals.

"It's never too late in fiction or in life to revise." Nancy Thayer

Give yourself permission to reflect backward a few months and then plan forward a few months. Lead yourself forward—you can't always wait for others to lead you. Prepare your heart to work for it. Following are some key questions to ask related to opportunities or potentially making changes (you can apply these either personally, professionally or both):

1) What's working in my life?

Take some credit for what you are doing well. Make a list and keep it with you. Write it in a journal if that's a tool that will help support you. Remember our Gem about praise and recognition? Praise from within is necessary. Look in your mirror and be your own cheerleader.

I am often guilty of yearning to go back in time, to being the cute little blondie that my grandparents and parents put on a beautiful pedestal.

Krista 'cute little blondie' 1974

We are responsible for our own internal pedestal, and must use it for our benefit, not our peril. I am my own worst critic, so hard on myself. My coach, my husband, and yes, my mother, are all keenly aware of this and are experts at calling me out on it. I find that many people share this trait with me, so I'm on a mission to help people stop beating themselves up. Tracking what you are doing well will assist you in articulating your skills when opportunity knocks and you are asked to share how you can contribute and make a difference.

2) What action(s) would take me closer to my commitments in the next 30 days?

Make a list of the things you need to do in order to draw closer to your commitments over the next month. But remember: "No" is a complete sentence. One of your actions may actually be saying no! Sometimes our best step forward is to make the choice to stop activities that do not serve us well. If you are over-committed somewhere, the time this commitment is taking in your life might be occupying the space you need to open up to provide for your new opportunity to knock. I am a habitual over-committer and people pleaser, especially in my volunteering and supporting others. It takes a lot of practice and effort to get comfortable saying "No."

3) What key choices or decisions must I make now, and what decisions can realistically wait?

This is one of my favorite places to arrive with coaching clients or with the volunteer boards I work with. Recall Mom's advice: "Resist the temptation to make everything URGENT! Be more productive and less stressed by avoiding the tyranny of the urgent in favor of the urgency of the important." Often, asking the question "Do you have to decide this today, or can it wait?" or "Do we have to decide this today or can it wait?" is one of the most empowering questions I can ask. It helps the decision maker evaluate the urgency or determine if there is no urgency after all. Then we're able to establish some more realistic priorities and put a stop to the "Analysis Paralysis" that can overwhelm us when there are too many decisions clamoring for our attention. Prioritizing your decisions and determining when to take any necessary actions or not will also influence opportunities, especially if those actions are linked to other people. Opportunity providers often appreciate a patient deliberator and thorough decision maker.

4) Who do I need to inform about what I want and need to do?
How can I help them, or invite them to help me?

Always remember: Most people love to help. My first day on the job at the country club, my boss sat me down in his office and prepared to impart some wisdom about how things operated. One of the statements he made that has stuck with me to this day is, "Ask for what you want 100% of the time." He was right. God did not give us the gift of mind reading, right? So it is up to us to ask for what we want and need. It is up to us to articulate where and when we need or want help. Apply this everywhere in your life.

Here's a personal example from my life with Scott. He and I both met as busy professionals in our 30's. I was divorced and had developed quite a sense of independence and self-sufficiency. He had been so dedicated to his career that he hadn't dated seriously or been compelled to commit his heart wholly, and was also very independent. Consequently when we began sharing a household, we didn't ask for what we wanted from each other easily because we continued to operate as two self-sufficient, independent people, but under the same roof. It took us a while, but we learned to ask for help when we needed it, and we learned to negotiate our independent, personal styles so that they complemented each other.

Then here's a professional example from my first years as a Lease Analyst in the commercial real estate space. I was hired to run lease analysis and return on investment for the landlord. Back then, we did this by entering numbers into a Lotus 123 spreadsheet. I knew *nothing* about Lotus or spreadsheets, and I'd never claimed proficiency with numbers, thanks to my scars from struggling with college calculus classes. I was open with my employers about what I did not know, and they said, "We'll teach you, it's easy!" And they did! I have become pretty darn good with spreadsheets. I enjoy using Excel now, and use just the basics to keep track of many numbers proficiently. Eventually, because I became well acquainted with what these ROI numbers represented with our landlords, I moved in more responsibilities beyond just "running the numbers all day." And this first opportunity as the Lease Analyst opened the doors for a really lovely career and my professional development in the commercial real estate business.

Opportunity may knock in the form of someone needing or asking for your help. Be prepared to give it and receive it. In offering help as well as being a gracious recipient of help, you have no idea what kinds of opportunity doors you may be opening by demonstrating your vast array of skills and "coachability."

For You to Say:

- When opportunity knocks...will you open the door? And will you determine the risk factors before making your decision?
- What if opportunity doesn't knock? How and where will you find it?
- Review your vision and goals and make an action plan. Prepare to work for it. Take ownership.

- Spend time volunteering and networking. Accept some volunteer positions or try out some jobs you know are temporary but may have a future. Be open to exploring.
- Develop a new skill or certification. Act!

Gem Number Fifteen: Practice Continuous Improvement

Begin with you.

MARY SAYS:

Successful people seek continuous improvement. This means they find ways to make changes in their approaches that increase satisfaction, achievement and joy. They seek ways to be in charge of every sector of life. Work at being more effective at home, at the dinner table, on the job, at church, as a parent, as a volunteer. Even when you are not the formally appointed leader, you can be an influencer for good. Increasing effectiveness of teams always leads to better, more satisfying outcomes for everyone.

In the retail business one of my bosses reminded us regularly: "The biggest danger of being good is not trying to be better."

My first take on this came at the university piano seminar where I compared myself to others in the group and realized I didn't belong there. Even though the critiques were painful, I *wanted* to belong there. I was determined to improve enough to make that happen.

At home today, I'm constantly rearranging furniture, thinking of new ways to store things so they are more convenient and better accessed. I just thrive on order and efficiency, so I constantly think of how I can do something faster, better, cheaper....

Following are seven skills that, when practiced faithfully, are *guaranteed* to promote continuous improvement. They were developed by Jack Zenger to create leadership effectiveness in business, but they have proven to be even more effective as a personal growth strategy. They work for me, and they work for people in every area of life.

1. Build your personal vision of the desired future. (Follow the instructions in Gem Two.) After you have done that, share it with those around you—make it a *shared* vision of the desired future. Recruit others to help you to achieve. Then remember the questions "Who will be with you?" and "What resources will I need?" Some of those will be human resources.

2. Be an excellent listener. Listening is such an important skill that we've devoted an entire chapter to it! So often in conversations, discussions or arguments, people aren't truly listening—there are only persons waiting their turn to talk. No one is listening to what is being said because everyone is mentally formulating his or her own comments! Being a good listener shows respect faster and more effectively than any other interaction. How do you know when you are a good listener? You give the speaker the full benefit of your attention. You maintain eye contact. You nod in encouragement. You ask clarifying questions...is this what I heard you say? Is this what you meant? I don't understand, can you tell me a little more about it? I can tell you have strong feelings about this—what happened to cause you to feel sad ... angry ... disappointed ... hurt, etc. And unless the person specifically asks your opinion, do not offer advice.

3. Enable strong followers. Believe in your team members, children, and others in relationships with you. Surround yourself with strong people. Children are our best opportunity to leave a legacy. Without strong successors, who will maintain the traditions, expand your business, make a difference, or send independent young people into the world?

Here are a few "How-To's":

- *Seek diversity in skills, style and worldviews.*
- *Value team members equally.* Value each person for his or her unique contributions.
- *Leaders look for what's right and praise it.* To be effective, 80% of feedback must be positive. This is not habitual for most of us. We are trained to look for what's wrong and fix it, rather than look for what's right and praise it. Consider the elementary school spelling test of fifty words. At the top of the page, usually in red, we read about two wrong! Never 48 correct...
- *Serve as coach, mentor, sometimes disciplinarian.* This includes difficult discussions like coaching for improved performance and providing consequences for unacceptable behaviors. Criticism for criticism's sake has no purpose. Criticism is detrimental unless it's coupled with ways to seek improvement.
- *Communicate expectations clearly.* Effective leaders make sure that family members, team members, or board members understand what is expected and accept the responsibility for completing their tasks in a way that helps those expectations to be met or exceeded.

- *Take responsibility for the results your team produces.* Don't take individual credit for great results, and never publicly place blame when the results are less than expected.

4. Keep a laser focus on the important stuff. Ask, "*What* is the problem?" Then move on to help figure out how to fix it. Never ask, "*Who* is the problem?" Resist the temptation to make everything URGENT! Be more productive and less stressed by avoiding the tyranny of the urgent in favor of the urgency of the important.

5. Accept responsibility for results. Have a passion for the mission and the goals. Have a mission statement that the family, the team, the group believes in, and repeat it often. "How does this fit in our mission statement?" is a critical question.

6. Expectations must be clear, and then let people figure out their own methods and processes for completion. These are *not* contradictory positions. Roll up your sleeves and work with the group.

7. Let people know how important they are to you—and your mission. Engage with other people, other family members, other members of the church group, school teachers and other parents, other team leaders in the company, other business owners, and other members of the community to better understand their position and to help them to understand yours.

8. Lead change. Talk about change in a way that shows the necessary change in the most positive light. How will this affect our vision of the desired future? Accepting change and its impact on the bigger picture are important considerations

for success. Status quo can be deadly. Provide honest feedback about how the individual and the team is viewed in the eyes of the larger world. Seek strategic information, develop networks to help gather feedback effectively. And as a parent, this helps rebut the argument "Everyone is doing it."

KRISTA SAYS:

The Gem of practicing continuous improvement is absolutely crucial, and one of the greatest DNA gifts passed along in my bloodline. It's right in there with the golf genes, my (nearly) perfect ear for music, and my McElhinney nose.

Mom and I have both mentioned the importance of being willingly open to acknowledge what we do not know. So with that in mind, what do you do when you acknowledge something you don't know? In my world, I get on a mission to "go find out," to dive in, to source new information, to figure it out. In other words, I begin with me, and I find a way to practice continuous improvement.

As a professional, I've pursued many means of continuing education and have enjoyed them all. Some professions may not require continuing education, but adding to your knowledge base and skill set is never a bad idea, and in my case, adding to my education and skills collection usually meant a quicker move up. A willingness to learn demonstrates dedication and taking ownership for your role, whatever it may be. Additional education almost always translates to improvement.

As a golfer I attended the PGA's business school, where we learned golf-specific business tools and teaching to equip us as golf facility professionals, business people, shop operators, golf instructors, turf grass growers and more. As a realtor, I set on a course to be a realtor with the "alphabet soup" of designations after my name: GRI, CRS, and ABR. Fortunately, I worked with a company who valued these designations and made it a priority to provide educational opportunities for its agents and associates. As a Rotarian, we have many opportunities for further learning and self-development, such as Rotary University, RILI (Rotary International Leadership Institute), district training for specific leadership roles such as Club President (President Elects Training), zone training for district leader roles, and much more. For professional coaching, I reviewed several options for coach training and certification before making the choice to attend the Core Essentials Program with Coach University. Just recently, in my desire to prepare for the next part of my desired future, I began my journey toward Viticulture and Enology Certification. My point is, I'm turning 50 this year and I'm still improving and intend to continuously improve the rest of my life. Like fine wine, I'm improving with age.

In your pursuit of Continuous Improvement, here are three words I encourage each person to embrace thoughtfully:

Intentional
Purposeful
Specific

Since 2009 I've been working with a personal and business coach. My message to myself was, "KK, if you want to be a good coach, you'd better be a good coachee, too." Over the years, through numerous conversations with my coach, the recurring theme included these three words. They now govern my entire personal foundation—with myself, my clients, my volunteer work, my life!

Intentional: Continuous improvement starting with me is Intentional. I take ownership of my intentions, and the vision of my desired future. I "set" an intention ahead of my beginnings or actions. For example, "I intend to complete Viticulture and Enology Certification with flying colors." Being intentional clarifies your purpose and holds you accountable to it.

Purposeful: Continuous improvement starting with me is Purposeful. I establish my purposes and reasons for wanting to improve. Being "on purpose" moves me in the direction beyond dreaming to goal setting, which makes my vision real. For example, "My purpose for completing Viticulture and Enology school is to have the knowledge of both grape-growing and winemaking so in the not so distant future Scott and I can make our shared dream of owning a vineyard and winery a reality."

Krista Harvesting Tempranillo Grapes 2014

Specific: Just as we see in the acronym S.M.A.R.T. (Specific, Measurable, Action-Oriented, Realistic, and Timely), you'll be far more successful in achieving your goals if you start with specific goals. As a planner and strategic thinker, I also get specific with the goal's outcomes: I must be specific with "by when?" and "how many?" or "how much?" With the gift of a great imagination I can see the future coming vividly to life in my mind. I must also be specific with others—team members, my stakeholders, my husband, family members, friends, and peers—so I state my vision, dreams, goals and challenges clearly and receive acknowledgement and acceptance so we all end up on the same page. For example: "I will complete my Viticulture and Enology certification by the conclusion of 2017, so I may begin practicing winemaking on a larger scale, and gain valuable hands-on experiences working with wineries and vineyard owners in the area, so my educational journey prepares me to begin seeking a location to establish the Hartman winery and vineyard by 2020." This intention is detailed and specific, and it encompasses the entire team.

Recently, I listened to a Marine give a talk about helping other Marines who are returning home wounded. This young man was severely wounded by an IED in Iraq, subsequently endured 46 operations, and experienced a recovery process beyond anything we could conceive of. He believes that helping his fellow Marines heal helps his ongoing healing. Now that's a commitment to Continuous Improvement, and was so inspirational to me. Hopefully we will all engage in our journeys of Continuous Improvement with the courage, dedication, and selflessness of this veteran.

For You to Say:

- Where can you identify your Continuous Improvement opportunities?
- How prepared are you to do the work?
- How will you practice leadership starting with yourself in your personal life?
- What places or parts of your life are you willing to engage in Continuous Improvements? And with whom?
- What will be your first steps?

Putting All the Gems Together

"Today is a Very Good Day."
~Winnie the Pooh

MARY SAYS:

For me, the Gems are like putting together a beautiful bracelet with gratitude linking the chain. Every day I find applications for them. I seek balance in my life. Kay and I spent many years working long hours, raising our children, and being deeply involved in our communities. This often left little time for the two of us to enjoy one another's company. Now is our time! The two months we take away from Iowa in the winter are sheer luxury—and fun.

Mary & Kay at the Masters 2011

I love writing. Writing a blog from time to time lowers my blood pressure. Any time I am inspired (or angry enough) I add to my blog at www.madameambassador.com. One rule, always "sleep" on a blog—never just "fire it off." Keeping in contact with friends and family through social media is a treat. Working with Krista on this book has been a wonderful experience. I hope the book will be read and valued by many people, but my experience in working with Krista to write it has been my reward enough.

Kay is fond of saying "everyone is happier when Mary is fully engaged." *True*. It is important to me to stay engaged and to continue to give back. These days I am much more selective as I choose projects and board experiences. Before leaving the country to serve as an Ambassador, I served on many boards and commissions. I said yes whenever I thought I could make a contribution. Leaving the country meant resigning from all those responsibilities. When I returned my calendar was a blank slate, and I decided to accept only those opportunities and invitations that reflected my first loves—culture, music and shared communication. So I serve on public broadcast and performing arts boards. I am a public speaker. Civility in public discourse and leadership skills are particular passions, so opportunities to speak on or become engaged in projects involving those two things appeal to me. I know I am happiest when there are more opportunities than I have time or energy to do.

I have learned to be mindful of my stamina and energy because I wear out faster than I used to. I enjoy the freedom to be spontaneous, so it is important to save my energy to do fun stuff when opportunities arise, and to exercise. If I had a do-over in my life, I would have started regular exercise much earlier. I now know how much better I feel when I commit to regular workouts.

Kay and I enjoy creating opportunities for our family to make memories by traveling together. Our next generations are fully engaged in careers, and our grandchildren are maturing into busy young adults as well. We invest energy and resources to create opportunities to stay connected by planning activities for all of us to be together. Hard to think of anything more important.

Most satisfying right now? Being free to choose how much and what kind of activity I will undertake. *No one controls my calendar!* There is no single focus of a job I need to show up for every day. It is the best of times! I have given myself permission to be nice to myself, to manage my involvement so I have time and energy to focus on the things I want to do and enjoy doing. I plan activities in that time management square that are neither important nor urgent. And I say no. As Krista has reminded me, "No is a complete sentence."

Least satisfying at this point? Accepting the fact that I do not have the stamina I once had. That may be a good thing. I continue to make too many calendar commitments just like I used to. It's hard for me to say no, and I try not to feel guilty about saying it so often, particularly when I think I could be helpful. It is a delight to know our kids and grandkids enjoy spending time with us. And to have so many opportunities to be engaged in meaningful activities at this stage of my life. I try to avoid "regular" stuff—i.e. things that happen every week and that would require my regular presence. It makes me cross when there is too much on the schedule. And I resent it when people say, "You should do this—after all you're retired." Yes, I am! I am retired after a 50+ year-career in business, politics, education, and community service. Kay and I raised two wonderful, successful children who are actively involved in their own careers, communities and families. I've earned the right to manage my own calendar—and to say yes and no at my own discretion. Retirement isn't about replicating the activities that filled my time before retirement. It's about using time responsibly, respecting my own desires and capabilities, and applying my energies to the activities that bring me joy, that give back to the community, and make a difference.

Finally, for me what ties the Gems together more than anything else is *gratitude*. Gratitude means not only being grateful for the gifts I have been given, it also means appreciating the opportunities I've had to use those gifts to make a difference. Sometime during each day I try to consider what I'm most grateful for on that particular day. And sometimes I find so much to be grateful for I feel overwhelmed! My list of gratitudes has grown exponentially as I've aged and can look back on a lifetime of blessings. One of my favorite songs describes it perfectly: "And I say to myself...it's a wonderful world."

In addition to the practice of gratitude, here are some of the things that never fail to make me happy and for which I am profoundly grateful.

Never doubting I am loved. I remember that no matter how much I love or am loved, God loves me more. I believe this is true of every person.

Good stewardship. I do my best to use my resources—time, talent and treasure—intelligently. I try to give more than I get—or at least come out even! Giving gives me pleasure, especially when it benefits others. On the other side of the coin, I try to avoid waste, and resist the temptation of reaching for every newer, shinier object that comes along.

Using power wisely. I do not fear having power; I welcome it. In fact I often seek more of it because power creates opportunities: to do more, to move an agenda forward, to make things happen, to right wrongs, to achieve! Whether I have authority or influence is unimportant. I am content to be a follower or a participant when things are getting done. When things are not getting done, I reconsider my involvement: Is this a good use of my time, talent, or treasure? Is the juice worth the squeeze? If no, then I move on. If yes, I become more assertive.

Remembering the times I made a difference. Those of us who enjoy the blessings of personal liberty, of growing up in a loving environment, and who appreciate our quality of life have a duty to give back. As Americans, we owe an extraordinary debt to those generations who brought us to the edge of this new and promised land. Their sacrifices not only bequeathed to us the invaluable legacy of a good life, but through wars and hard times, they have kept our values alive. It is our task to preserve those values and to pass them on to future generations—in America and throughout the world.

KRISTA SAYS:
Our Gems take on greater and greater meaning for me the more time passes and the more I reflect on how my life and my values have been framed or shaped by them. I cherish my family history and their many, many traditions.

Longevity. In my immediate family lineage there is longevity. Longevity in living, longevity in marriages and relationships, longevity in Iowa. Sharing the gifts and values of my family truly means the world to me, and one of my primary motivations in life is the desire to share the wealth of wisdom that's been passed down to me over a lovely lifetime spent with my very special family. Am I saying my family has the patent on doing everything perfectly? No way... but I would say we have an excellent model for growing and innovating together. I have been shown, been a part of, and contributed to an awesome legacy that is represented by the fifteen Gems.

Now, **this legacy is my foundation and my responsibility to carry forward**. I've incorporated much about these Gems and their meaning into the new KK Hartman Partners website (www.kkhartman.com) and our business plans for the future.

Scott's Rock. For her wedding toast to us and prayer ahead of our reception dinner, Scott's mom, Kathy, arrived at the front of the room with a big rock. When Scott was just a little guy he apparently insisted on toting this big rock back to the house in his red wagon while Kathy was on a walk with him on their rural property in Wisconsin. It's a beautiful piece of limestone. On this rock she had a small brass plate affixed with the inscription: "Matthew 7:24-27 9-28-03." This is our wedding date and the reference to a passage in the Gospel of Matthew.

Scott and his Matthew 7: 24-27 Rock September 28, 2003

The parable appears as part of the Sermon on the Mount, and is as follows: "Everyone therefore who hears these words of mine, and does them, I will liken him to a wise man, who built his house on a rock. The rain came down, the floods came, and the winds blew, and beat on that house; and it didn't fall, for it was founded on the rock. Everyone who hears these words of mine, and doesn't do them will be like a foolish man, who built his house on the sand. The rain came down, the floods came, and the winds blew, and beat on that house; and it fell—and great was its fall."

Now over the years in my life, I have built a few "sand castles"—I've shared about a few of them within these pages. Life is never without its share of sand castles, which sooner or later get blown over, flooded, or beaten down. But at the end of the day, I've always been able to return to and rely on the foundation created by the Kramer family Gems. If it's a situation with a job, a relationship, an opportunity, a risk, a chance for change or growth…pick any scenario and these Gems are applicable and provide failsafe support! They've always been there to inform me or equip me when I need them.

They can do the same for you.

Mission. Through the support of the Kramer family Gems, the Kramer family itself, and marrying a man who is a part of a family with a highly complementary value system, **I've discovered my true purposes, strengths, and passions.** I've made it a mission to help others learn that change can be navigated in a positive way, and I've made it part of my purpose to help people uncover the positives in what they perceive to be negatives.

I've learned to develop a healthy balance of "be yourself, be different, be willing to take responsibility for yourself and your actions," and be alone if alone seems to be a stop along my journey.

I've learned to look forward to the intersection of choice and change, knowing that with choices and changes come risks. I've successfully managed change over and over, I've strategized and prepared.

I've learned that teaching someone else a skill means two people are learning, because in teaching I am still learning and growing too. I just love this. It brings me a great deal of joy. Even if it's something simple to me, like baking cookies, learning a chip shot at the practice green, or making a difficult decision, **it brings me joy to be a teacher by illustration out there in the world.**

My life has pretty much been delightful, and like Mom I often find myself overwhelmed with gratitude. When someone asks me how I'm doing, I like to respond that there's never a dull moment,

I am happy, I am spoiled and blessed, and that someone should slap me if I whine or complain.

I'm really proud to be the wife of an amazing man who "gets" me, who understands my entrepreneurial spirit and my passion for volunteering and helping people. We celebrated our 11-year anniversary last fall and are anticipating many more. We are adventurers. Scott is Visioneering right alongside me as we bring to life our shared dream of becoming winemakers, opening a winery and vineyard.

I'm really proud to be the daughter of a powerful and successful woman, and an unfailingly supportive dad. There are many things about my parents that make me proud, but at the top of the list are: 1) My parents remain happily married after 57 years together. They are healthy. And they enjoy a robust retirement together, and 2) My mother is a former U.S. Ambassador and her journey to get there is awesome (How many daughters have the privilege of saying this?) and 3) My father is just the most special example of an awesome husband and human being.

I am what I am and I am who I am because of the deep and powerful influence of the Kramer family Gems. In my opinion, I've been given a great model to follow. I am so honored to share this precious legacy with you in these pages. And I can't emphasize enough, *I am grateful.*

The Family Who's Who

*Throughout the book we have referred to friends and
family members.
Here's more you might want to know about each one.*

Mary Kramer - pianist, teacher, human resources officer, state senator, Senate President, U.S. Ambassador, author, public speaker. Wife of Kay and mother of Kent and Krista.

Kay Kramer - trumpet player, bandleader, teacher, college professor, marketer, government relations guru, volunteer, Rotarian. Husband of Mary and father of Kent and Krista.

Kent Kramer - son of Mary and Kay, musician, Christian business leader and communications expert, financial counselor, business partner. Husband of Kimberley and father of Kelsey, Kallen, Karsen and Kennedy.

Kim Kramer - pianist, vocalist, teacher, composer. Wife of Kent and mother of Kelsey, Kallen, Karsen and Kennedy.

Kelsey Kramer McGinnis - daughter of Kent and Kim, University of Iowa graduate student, working at the U of I Department of Human Rights. Married to KC McGinnis November 2013.

KC McGinnis - University of Iowa graduate student, freelance photojournalist, seeking a master's degree in journalism.

Kallen Kramer Hawkinson - daughter of Kent and Kim, University of Iowa graduate, communications manager at Christian Heritage Schools in North Liberty Iowa. Married to Eric Hawkinson August 2013.

Eric Hawkinson - University of Iowa graduate student in communications at the UI School of Public Health, seeking a master's degree in urban planning.

Krista Kramer Hartman - daughter of Mary and Kay, musician, professional golfer, photographer, commercial and residential realtor, communications expert, serial entrepreneur, business coach and consultant, Rotarian, future wine maker, wife of Scott Hartman.

Scott Hartman - Wisconsin native, logistics, commercial real estate, business leader, marketing and sales training expert, coach, community volunteer, future grape grower, husband of Krista.

———

Ross Barnett - Iowa farm boy, athlete, coach, educator, soil conservationist. Mary's dad.

Geneva McElhinney Barnett - one of the McElhinney "girls," schoolteacher, and dietitian. Mary's mother.

———

Cyril Kramer - small business owner, grocer, investor, world traveler. Kay's dad.

Wilma Kramer - farm girl, teacher, community caregiver. Kay's mother.

Carol Kramer Johnson - small town girl, studied abroad, world traveler, environmentalist, married to Ken Johnson and mother of Jeffrey (and Kaye) Loralyn (and Jim) and Rosalyn, grandmother of eight, great grandmother of two, Kay's sister.

Nancy Kramer Graham - small town girl, musician, teacher, married to Dr. Michael Graham, mother of Christopher and Kevin (and Trish), grandmother of six, Kay's sister.

The "McElhinney girls," aka Geneva and her sisters - Aunt Isabelle (married to Uncle Ed Lotz), Aunt Frances (married to Uncle Walter Stang), and Aunt Ethel (married to Dr. Ralph Hart).

The "McElhinney brothers" - Uncle Clyde (married to Aunt Latha) and Uncle Elburn (married to Aunt Murray).

The McElhinney cousins by the dozens: the Johnsons, Tackenburgs, Galloways, Lotzs, Harts, Hastings...

The Rosonkes - MaryAnn and Dr. Dick: BFF's to Mary and Kay for 45 years.

Patty Kripal Thomas - BFF to Krista since January 1976, when the two became friends in third grade at Rolling Green Elementary School.

Kramer Family Recipes

APPETIZERS & SAVORIES

Hot Cheese Dip
Cranberry Baked Brie
French Onion Tart
Swiss Cheese Puffs

SOUPS

Butternut Squash Soup
Chili
Split Pea Soup
Kansas City Steak Soup
Chef Glen's Shrimp Bisque

SALADS

MaryAnn's Mandarin Tossed Salad with Toasted Almonds
Kimberly's Great Salad Idea
Butter Lettuce with Meyer Lemon Vinaigrette
Field Greens with Blue Cheese, Green Apple, Almonds, Green
Onions and Champagne Vinaigrette
Asian Chicken Salad with crispy Chow Mein Noodles and Sesame
Soy Dressing

BIG PLATES

Julia Child's Poached Chicken
Coq Au Vin
Beef Bourguignon
Sesame Ginger Pork Platter
This Is It Meatloaf

SIDE PLATES

Twice Baked Potatoes
Speedy Scalloped Potatoes
Meyer Lemon Parmesan Risotto
French Green Beans 3 Ways
Kimberly's Sweet Potato Soufflé

DESSERTS

Aunt Esther's Devil's Cake
Grandma Wilma's Pear Peach Custard Pie
The Bell File Chocolate Pudding
Hartman Limoncello Cheesecake
Ana Jorgenson's Rolled Sugar Cookies

Appetizers & Savories

HOT CHEESE DIP

Mary and Krista Say: We both usually make this recipe once (maybe twice) a year. When you attend either the Kramer or Hartman annual Christmas or New Year's Open House this is a staple on the table of beautiful foods we enjoy sharing. This is not a recipe for the calorie counters.

INGREDIENTS

1 pound ground beef
1 pound hot pork sausage
2 onions, roughly chopped
3 tomatoes, roughly chopped
1 small can diced green chilies
2 pounds Velveeta

DIRECTIONS

In a large stockpot or soup pan, over medium heat, brown the ground beef, sausage and onions together. Cook thoroughly enough to let any potential grease cook off. (If you want you can tamp any grease remaining on the surface with paper towels.)

Add the tomatoes and green chilies and cook until simmering.

Reduce heat to low.

Cut the Velveeta into 1-inch cubes and add by the handful, gradually stirring and stirring until melted and smooth. Remove from heat.

Serve with tortilla chips.

Present in a "hot" pan, small crock pot, or fondue set-up with minimal heat.

If, after your party you have any leftover, it freezes well. We usually save to enjoy during a bowl game in January.

TIPS, HINTS & EXTRAS
To make quickly:

Use 3 cups frozen chopped onions (drained).

Use 3 cans petite diced tomatoes w/chilies (drained).

If you use Light Velveeta, you cannot tell the difference.

This makes a lot of dip; you can freeze in small batches.

CRANBERRY BAKED BRIE

Krista says: This is a delightful warm appetizer or buffet table item for Thanksgiving, Christmas and other autumn, harvest or winter celebrations. It looks and tastes scrumptious.

INGREDIENTS

Cranberry Relish:
1.5 packages fresh cranberries (about 3 cups)
3/4 cup packed light brown sugar
2/3 cup dried currants
1/3 cup water
1/8 teaspoon allspice
1/8 teaspoon cardamom
1/8 teaspoon ground cloves
1/8 teaspoon ground ginger or finely minced fresh ginger
1/8 teaspoon dry mustard

Brie:
3 (8.8 ounce) Brie Cheese Wheels or
1 (2.2 pound) Brie Cheese Wheel

Cracked Pepper Water Crackers
Simple Water Crackers

French baguette cut in ½ inch rounds

Apple or pear slices

DIRECTIONS

Combine all relish Ingredients in a saucepan (2 qt. is a good size). Cook over medium to medium-high heat, stirring regularly, until you begin to hear cranberries popping (usually about 5-7 minutes).

Let cool to room temperature. Cover pan and chill for 3-4 hours.

20 minutes ahead of serving time preheat oven to 300°.

With a sharp knife cut out a circle of rind from the top of the cheese wheel, leaving a 1/4-1/2 inch rind outlining the top of the brie.

Spray an oven to tabletop pie plate or quiche dish with cooking oil spray, or smear lightly with butter. Place 1 8.8 oz. Brie wheel in the center and spread 1/3 cranberry relish over the cheese. (If using 2.2 lb. Brie, spread all relish over the cheese.) Bake approximately 10 minutes, or until softening.

Let cool slightly, present on a platter with crackers, fruit slices, or bread.

Bake additional 8.8 oz. Brie wheels at your pace to replenish your platter. Or freeze the relish and save for another occasion.

TIPS, HINTS & EXTRAS
Drizzle lemon juice on apple/pear slices to prevent browning.

Use a fine cheese zester/grater to get your ginger finely minced if using fresh.

Cranberries are mostly seasonal and aren't often available. Buy some extra October to December and freeze in case you'll want to make this when cranberries aren't in season. Or, if you're fortunate, sometimes cranberries can be found with frozen fruits. (Be sure to drain off any liquid after thawing.)

FRENCH ONION TART

Krista says: *As part of my "go to with confidence" dinner menu, you'll find this savory tart is a lovely starter to any dinner party. It's easy to prepare and always a hit.*

INGREDIENTS

Filling:
2 large sweet onions sliced in thin rings
2 strips Applewood smoked bacon
½ cup grated Gruyere or Swiss cheese
1 large egg yolk
½ cup heavy cream
Fresh nutmeg or nutmeg grinder
Pepper to taste

Crust:
1 already prepared pie crust from the refrigerated section of the grocery store

DIRECTIONS

Follow the directions for time and temperature to pre-bake crust unfilled in your tart pan. (A Pyrex pie dish, or ceramic quiche dish works well, as does a tart pan with a removable bottom.) Use either foil or parchment paper to line the crust, and prevent puffing using pie weights or a package of dried beans.

To make the filling, start cooking the bacon in a large sauté pan using medium to medium-high heat. As the bacon begins to brown add the onions and pepper to taste.

Sauté until the onions brown nicely (about 10-15 minutes). Remove the bacon and strain the onions gently, tossing to cool and remove bacon grease.

In a large bowl or 8 cup measuring cup whisk the egg yolk together with the cream. Add onions and cheese.

Grind nutmeg on top of the baked crust, then spoon the filling mixture into the crust.

Place tart pan on a cookie sheet and bake at 375 degrees for about 25 minutes or until tart is brown on top. Remove from the oven and cool slightly (5 minutes) before cutting and serving.

Serves 6-8

SWISS CHEESE PUFFS

Mary says: *Another savory appetizer that's always a hit at our parties. And in our earlier years, this was an elegant, yet inexpensive item to serve.*

Krista says: *For many years while I was at home I always looked forward to helping make this. It's especially fun as the host to wander around with an elegant tray of these and share them with party guests when they are just cool enough after having been under the broiler.*

INGREDIENTS

Spread:
1 (1 ½ cup) package finely/gourmet shredded Swiss cheese
3-5 tablespoons mayo (your taste & texture preference)
½ teaspoon Worcestershire sauce
1 tablespoon dried minced onion
1 tablespoon dried parsley
Dash or two of white pepper

Party loaf or mini loaf of sliced pumpernickel

DIRECTIONS

Start broiler and position over rack about ¾ to 2/3 toward the top of oven.

In a large bowl or 8-cup measuring cup use a small spatula to mix together all the spread Ingredients.

Spread cheese mixture on pumpernickel slices (about 1-2 teaspoons per piece) and place a sheet pan or cookie sheet.

Place under hot broiler until cheese bubbles and begins to slightly brown. This happens quickly so be cautious not to step away from your broiler for too long.

Let cool slightly (5 minutes) transfer to a serving tray and share with guests while warm.

Makes 20-24 toasted puffs.

Soups

BUTTERNUT SQUASH SOUP

Krista says: When Scott and I were first married and wanted to host Thanksgiving dinners, we wanted to shift from the habit of filling up on traditional snacks like chips and dips, etc. whilst watching football games, and instead we introduced the idea of enjoying a lunch of soup choices and a salad during half time of the first Thanksgiving Day ball game. This gave us all afternoon to look forward to the traditional turkey dinner, without the tendency to nosh on junk all day. In the same spirit of my great aunties and grandma Geneva who developed a "This Is It Meat Loaf," we've worked on creating our favorite squash soup recipe.

INGREDIENTS

2 pounds butternut squash, cubed
2 cups diced sweet yellow onions
1 cup diced carrots
1 cup diced celery (leaves are good, too)

1.5 sticks unsalted butter
1 cup flour

3 teaspoons ground sage
2 tablespoons ground thyme
½ teaspoon nutmeg
White pepper to taste
Salt to taste

2 quarts unsalted either chicken or vegetable broth (or combo)

1 cup Crème fraîche

DIRECTIONS

In a large soup pot (non-stick **not** suggested) over medium to medium-high heat melt butter. Sauté onions, carrots and celery with the squash until browning slightly.

Reduce heat to medium low and add sage and thyme. Stir to coat the vegetables. Cook another 5 minutes.

Gradually incorporate flour so all vegetables are coated with a flour paste. Add broth gradually to avoid lumps and simmer for 1 hour or until the squash breaks apart when stuck with a paring knife.

Remove from heat and cool slightly.

Use an emulsion blender to puree the mixture until smooth, directly in the soup pot.

Return to low heat. Add crème fraiche, nutmeg, white pepper and salt.

Serves 12+ depending upon your portion sizes. Freezes well in small batches.

TIPS, HINTS & EXTRAS
Most often the emulsion blender tolerant of hot food processing is a metal attachment, thus the suggestion not to use a non-stick pot.

You could also use either a food processor or blender to puree the squash/veg mixture in small batches. Or if your emulsion blender is plastic, cool your vegetable and broth mixture for a longer time. Use caution to cool the mixture enough so handling isn't uncomfortable and so you won't melt any heat-sensitive plastic appliance pieces. (From Krista's lessons learned). ☺

Sour cream or heavy whipping cream work well in the same quantities.

Depending upon your taste, experiment with sage and thyme leaves using an herb diffuser or sachet.

GARNISH IDEAS
Drizzled truffle oil
Crispy pancetta pieces
Smoked chicken or turkey pieces
Mushrooms sautéed in butter and sherry

CHILI

Krista says: A bubbling stew pot wafting savory aromas throughout the house on a Saturday or Sunday afternoon, especially during the fall and winter seasons, is always a welcome, comforting experience. Our family has prepared chili many different ways over the years, from something as simple as browned ground beef combined with a can of tomato chunks seasoned with green peppers and chili fixings, to a can of chili beans in mild or hot chili sauce plus leftover V-8 juice, to experimenting with adding chocolate chips, varying the meats, and more. Following is a good basic, hearty chili recipe. We encourage the "little bit of this and little bit of that" doctoring it up style when making chili.

INGREDIENTS

3 pounds ground lean beef (ground turkey works just as well)
1 large yellow onion, roughly chopped
3 stalks celery, roughly chopped
1 green bell pepper, seeded and roughly chopped
1 red bell pepper, seeded and roughly chopped
2 tablespoons minced garlic
1 cup beer
¼ cup chili powder
1 tablespoon Worcestershire sauce
1 tablespoon dried oregano
2 teaspoons ground cumin
2 teaspoons hot pepper sauce
1 teaspoon dried basil
1 teaspoon fine ground sea salt
1 teaspoon black pepper

1 teaspoon cayenne pepper
4 cubes beef bouillon (or 4 tablespoons reduced sodium beef base)
2 (28 ounce) cans petite-diced fire roasted tomatoes with juice
3 (15 ounce) cans chili beans (drained), such as dark red kidney
beans
1 (15 ounce) can chili beans in spicy sauce
1 (6 ounce) can tomato paste
1 teaspoon white sugar (dark brown sugar, honey or agave nec-
tar work well, too)

DIRECTIONS

In a deep soup pot over medium-high heat brown ground beef until
no longer pink. Add onions and celery and cook another 5-7 minutes.
Add green and red pepper plus garlic and cook another 3-5 minutes.

You should have little to no fat from the protein remaining, but at
this point if you'd like to, reduce heat to low and carefully tamp
grease with a wrinkled paper towel to remove.

Add the beer and allow its liquid to absorb and reduce/cook off. Add
the beef base and all spices. Allow the seasonings to coat the beef and
vegetables evenly. Add the diced tomatoes with juice. Return heat to
medium-high and add the remaining Ingredients. Bring to a boil,
then reduce to a simmer and let stew for at least an hour or more.

Serve with oyster crackers, shredded cheddar cheese, sour cream and
diced onions. This is a great "make the day before" soup where the
flavors improve with time.

TIPS, HINTS AND EXTRAS
For less spicy chili, use less chili powder—2-3 tablespoons—and use canned chili beans with mild sauce.

For increased heat and spiciness, add 1 small can diced green chilies.

ADDITIONAL GARNISH IDEAS
Thinly sliced banana bell pepper rings
Macaroni and Cheese
Semi-Sweet Chocolate Chips
Frito's chips or tortilla strips

SPLIT PEA SOUP

Krista says: *Honestly, no Thanksgiving, Christmas or Easter celebration comes and goes without an Iowa ham being served. This means there's always a good ham bone to be used for Split Pea Soup. The bags of dried split peas you purchase at the grocery store provide a good foundational recipe for this hearty soup. We put our signature additions into this soup over the years. Frankly it's probably a little different preparation each time.*

INGREDIENTS

2 pound dried split peas
1 Iowa ham bone
2 cups roughly chopped ham bits & pieces
3 tablespoons unsalted butter
3 tablespoons olive oil
2 cups roughly chopped sweet onion
1 cup roughly chopped celery, including leaves
1 cup cut carrots (leave as round cuts)
4 tablespoons chopped garlic
1-2 teaspoons black pepper (generosity is up to you)
8 cups unsalted chicken stock or broth (half and half works well too)
4 bay leaves
4 springs fresh thyme tied in a bundle with kitchen twine or placed in herb diffuser or sachet

DIRECTIONS

Place ham bone and 2 bay leaves in large soup pot with water to cover and bring to a boil. Reduce heat and let simmer, stirring occasionally, for 1 hour. Remove from heat, gently lift bone from liquids, allowing any meat pieces to fall into soup pot. Discard bone.

In a large soup pot, with medium-high heat, melt the butter with the olive oil. Add onions and sauté for about 3 minutes, add celery, carrots and garlic, and sauté until carrots start to soften, about 3 minutes. Add the ham bone liquid and meat pieces, plus 2 cups ham bits and pieces and continue to cook on medium-high heat until Ingredients begin to brown slightly. Add dried peas and 1 teaspoon black pepper; incorporate with the soup and stir together about 1-2 minutes. Add stock, bay leaf and thyme sprigs. Bring to a boil and reduce heat to low. Let simmer for 2 hours or longer if desired or until peas are tender. Add small amounts of water if needed to prevent soup from becoming pasty or dry. The thickness of this hearty soup is up to you.

Remove thyme sprigs and bay leaves. Serves 12+ depending upon your portion sizes. Freezes well in small batches.

TIPS, HINTS & EXTRAS
Salt is hardly needed. If your ham was a honey glazed or smoked ham, it will retain salt from those preparations.

This is a great "make the day before" soup where the flavors improve with time.

KANSAS CITY STEAK SOUP (PLAZA III)

Krista says: *A fond memory I love to share about the Plaza III was one evening while waiting for a table with Mom and Dad and enjoying a glass of wine in the bar, we made a request of the pianist to play Gershwin's "Rhapsody in Blue." Without hesitation this obviously quite accomplished young man provided a virtuoso performance of this beautiful composition. He received a standing ovation from the bar patrons and likely the largest tip to a musician's tip jar Kay Kramer ever made.*

Mary Says: *Aunt Ethel Hart provided this recipe from the famous steak house, Plaza III in Kansas City.*

INGREDIENTS

1 stick unsalted butter
1 cup flour
½ gallon of water
2 cups sautéed ground beef (about 1 pound)
1 cup chopped yellow onion
1 cup chopped carrots
1 cup chopped celery
2 cups frozen mixed vegetables
1 (15 ounce) can chopped tomatoes
2 teaspoons beef bouillon granules
1 teaspoons black pepper

DIRECTIONS

In a 2-quart or larger saucepan, place onion, carrots and celery. Fill with enough water to cover at the surface. Bring to a boil and remove from heat. Cool slightly and drain water.

In a sauté pan, brown ground beef and drain off grease.

In a large soup pot melt butter. Use a whisk to incorporate flour like a roux and gradually stir in water. Add browned beef and parboiled vegetables, along with frozen veg, tomatoes, bouillon and pepper.

Bring to a boil, stirring often, then reduce heat to simmer and cook until vegetables are done.

TIPS, HINTS & EXTRAS
Does not need salt.

Freezes well in small batches.

CHEF GLEN'S SHRIMP BISQUE (IN CHEF GLEN'S OWN WORDS)

Mary says: *Chef Glen served memorable meals at the Ambassador's residence in Barbados. When asked for the recipe for his Shrimp Bisque, he had to stop and think, and then made one up on the spot. During her second stay in Barbados, a then six-year-old Kennedy announced her second favorite food was shrimp bisque, right behind French fries.*

INGREDIENTS

Shelled shrimp, ½ pound
Tomato paste, 2 tablespoons
Onions, 2 large
Celery, 1 stalk
Thyme, 1 sprig
Marjoram, 1 sprig
Fish stock or water, and heavy cream
Butter, 2 tablespoons and flour, 2 tablespoons (roux)

DIRECTIONS

Sauté shrimp and other Ingredients together.

Add stock or water. Come to a boil and reduce for 20 minutes.

Blend all together and strain.

Thicken with roux and 4 tablespoons heavy cream.

TIPS, HINTS & EXTRAS

This is a great memory from Barbados. If we don't find fresh thyme or marjoram, ¼ teaspoon dried of each work pretty well.

We make a best guess for the amount of stock. Usually a quart works well. Sometimes it was probably adjusted depending on how many people were expected for dinner.

Salads

Krista says: The genes we've been gifted with mean we're equipped with a McElhinney nose, or the gift of determining smells and tastes in a hypersensitive way. Or at least we think so. So dissecting foods in restaurants has become a little game or hobby of ours, especially with salads.

MARYANN'S MANDARIN TOSSED SALAD
WITH TOASTED ALMONDS

Mary says: Our dear family friend MaryAnn created this easy-to-prepare, fresh and flavorful salad that's a wonderful follow-up after the soup course or for the first flavors you're offering your guests when they've just arrived at your beautiful dinner table.

INGREDIENTS

Dressing:
1 teaspoon salt with a pinch of black pepper
½ teaspoon Tabasco sauce
¼ cup white sugar
¼ cup tarragon vinegar
½ cup canola oil

In the Salad Bowl:
1 head iceberg lettuce (washed/torn)
2 cups finely chopped celery
2 tablespoons finely chopped fresh parsley
4 green onions tops, sliced
2 (11 ounce) cans mandarin oranges (drained)

Garnish with Toasted Almonds:
½ cup slivered almonds
4 tablespoons unsalted butter

DIRECTIONS

In a small sauté pan, melt butter and add almonds. Gently toast on medium-low heat for 2-3 minutes.

In a jar with a lid you can secure for shaking, combine all the Ingredients and shake well until blended.

In a salad serving bowl place lettuce first and top with celery, parsley, green onions and oranges. Add the dressing and gently toss.

Sprinkle the warm toasted almonds on top.

Serve at once.

Serves 8 to 10.

KIMBERLY'S GREAT SALAD IDEA: SPRING MIX WITH STRAWBERRIES AND ALMOND VINAIGRETTE

Mary says: When Jell-O was falling out of favor, and our family trend was to pay closer attention to adding fresh vegetables to our meals and gatherings, Kimberly had the perfect contemporary replacement for me.

INGREDIENTS

Dressing:
½ cup canola oil
2 tablespoons sugar
2 tablespoons white wine vinegar
½ teaspoon salt (a couple cranks on your sea salt grinder)
1 teaspoon almond extract

In the Salad Bowl:
1 package of Spring Mix
¼ to ½ cup fresh chopped parsley
1 cup sliced fresh strawberries

Garnish with Glazed Almonds:
¼ cup sliced almonds
2 tablespoons white sugar

DIRECTIONS

In medium to large sauté pan over high heat, add almonds and sprinkle with sugar. Stir constantly until sugar melts. This process happens rapidly; use caution not to overcook and/or burn. The melted sugar is very hot; transfer nuts to cool completely on plate pre-sprayed lightly with cooking spray. Once cooled, break into bite-sized pieces.

In a jar with a lid you can secure for shaking, combine all the dressing Ingredients and shake well until blended.

In a salad serving bowl layer Spring Mix, parsley, and strawberries. Add the dressing and gently toss.

Sprinkle with glazed almonds on top and serve.

YUM!

SIMPLE SALAD: BUTTER LETTUCE WITH MEYER LEMON VINAIGRETTE

Krista says: Scott and I started growing dwarf Meyer Lemon trees in half wine barrels shortly after we moved to Dallas. We've become fond of making many different types of foods using Meyer Lemons.

INGREDIENTS

Dressing:
4 tablespoons Meyer lemon juice (about 2 large Meyers)
4 tablespoons extra virgin olive oil
Freshly ground sea salt to taste
1 teaspoon traditional or white balsamic or red wine vinegar (red gives the most bite)
1-2 teaspoons mayo (optional depending upon your taste and diet)
1 teaspoon honey
2 cloves crushed garlic

In the Salad Bowl:
Torn Butter Lettuce (washed and paper towel dried)
Shaved Parmesan
Freshly cracked pepper

DIRECTIONS

In a jar with a lid you can secure for shaking, combine all the Ingredients and shake well until blended. (If you decide to go with the mayo option, using a hand blender to mix together works beautifully.)

TIPS, HINTS & EXTRAS

The ratio of lettuce to servings is roughly 1 generous handful for a small side salad.

Use about 1 to 1 ½ tablespoons dressing per person.

Gently sprinkle shaved Parmesan after dressing.

Be generous with your freshly cracked pepper.

Other additions to try:
Slivered almonds
Crispy pancetta pieces

We end up with lots of extra lemon juice each growing season, so I juice the lemons and freeze in ice cube trays. One cube is 2-3 tablespoons and works beautifully for quickly whipping together this lovely salad dressing.

The store-prepared crushed garlic is a great shortcut for this kind of recipe. Keep a jar in your refrigerator.

THE SALAD. FIELD GREENS/SPRINGS MIX
WITH CHAMPAGNE VINAIGRETTE

Krista says: As we established the soup and salad tradition for Thanksgiving meals, this salad became known as "The Salad." And having made it up as a copycat from a couple of favorite restaurants in Chicago, I had to create a recipe to share with the family.

INGREDIENTS

Dressing:
2 tablespoons high quality Dijon mustard
2 tablespoons champagne vinegar
6 tablespoons extra-virgin olive oil
Salt and freshly ground pepper to taste

In the Salad Bowl:
Field greens/spring mix etc.
Thinly sliced cored green apple (skin remains)
4 green onions diced (cut to the end of the green, save the white/bulb end for something else you're cooking later)
Slivered almonds
Crumbled blue or Gorgonzola cheese

DIRECTIONS

In a jar with a lid you can secure for shaking, combine the first 3 Ingredients and shake well until blended. (Using a hand blender to mix together works well, especially if you double or triple the recipe to serve a larger group.)

Add 1-2 handfuls green per person to a large salad serving bowl; layer slices of green apple, diced green onions, and slivered almonds.

Drizzle 1 to 1 ½ tablespoons dressing per person you're serving on top of the salad. Toss gently with tongs or salad servers. Add desired amount of blue cheese crumbles and gently toss again.

TIPS, HINTS & EXTRAS
Use kitchen shears or herb scissors to cut the green onions.

This is fun to serve on salad plates pre-chilled in the freezer for about 30 minutes.

I fell in love with Maile Dijon whilst in France. It's a delightful Dijon to use for this preparation. I don't recommend the Dijon with the coarse ground mustard seeds.

ASIAN CHICKEN SALAD WITH CRISPY CHOW MEIN NOODLES AND SESAME-GINGER VINAIGRETTE

Krista says: Dad and I have been fans of using soy sauce in many food preparations. We like the saltiness and Asian flare it provides. In the late 90's there seemed to be a surge in popularity with a version of Asian Chicken Salads at casual restaurants. This is my copycat version.

INGREDIENTS

Chicken Marinade:
¾ cup lemon juice (about 4 lemons)
¾ cup olive oil
2 tablespoons low sodium soy sauce
1 teaspoon Asian spice blend of your choice
1 teaspoon finely ground sea salt
1 teaspoon ground black pepper
2 lbs. boneless chicken breast, no skins

Dressing:
2 tablespoons rice wine vinegar
2 tablespoons low sodium soy sauce
2 tablespoons honey
½ teaspoon dark toasted sesame oil
1 teaspoon sesame seeds
2 teaspoons grated fresh ginger
4 tablespoons canola oil

In the Salad Green Bowl:
Torn red & green lettuces

Green onions, diced
Slivered almonds
Chow Mein noodles
Snow pea pods, steamed (optional)
Edamame, steamed and beans removed from skins (optional)
Carrot, slivers or shredded
Green pepper slivers
Store prepared pot stickers

DIRECTIONS

For the marinade, in a blender or large bowl, whisk/blend together first six Ingredients.

Pour over chicken, cover and marinate 4-6 hours or overnight.

Grill chicken about 10 minutes per side until just cooked. Cool slightly, and slice diagonally into strips.

For the dressing, in jar with a lid you can secure for shaking, combine all Ingredients and shake well until blended. (Using a hand blender to mix together works beautifully, especially if you double or triple the recipe to serve a larger group.)

Add 1-2 handfuls green per person to a large salad serving bowl, diced green onions, slivered almonds and any of the optional veg.

Drizzle 1 to 1 ½ tablespoons dressing per person on top of the salad, toss gently with tongs or salad servers.

Layer chicken strips on top and serve.

TIPS, HINTS & EXTRAS
Use kitchen shears or herb scissors to cut the green onions.

The store-prepared crushed ginger is a great shortcut for this kind of recipe. Keep a jar in your refrigerator.

This is also excellent using the Ginger Glazed Pork Tenderloin (recipe to come) in lieu of the grilled chicken.

Big Plates

JULIA CHILD'S POACHED CHICKEN WITH MUSHROOMS

Mary says: Early in our marriage, I decided I needed a really great menu that I could produce easily for guests—even with kids underfoot or late arrivals, this menu worked. It consists of chicken, a well-seasoned rice casserole, frozen peas seasoned with minced onion, thyme and parsley, and a salad. I used to make an apricot orange Jell-O, but Jell-O has fallen from favor, so now I make Kim's Strawberry Salad or MaryAnn's Mandarin Tossed Salad with Toasted Almonds. I found the recipe for this chicken dish in Julia's cookbook.

This was my first attempt at "gourmet" cooking. I got so much applause I think it led me down the path to believe I could cook anything!

INGREDIENTS

4-5 pound frying chicken, cut into pieces (bone-in)
4 tablespoons unsalted butter
Salt and pepper
3 tablespoons flour
3 cups chicken stock
1 cup dry white wine
1 tablespoon parsley
1 bay leaf
¼ teaspoon dried thyme

½ pound fresh sliced mushrooms
2 tablespoons unsalted butter
1 tablespoon lemon juice
1 tablespoon water or white wine

DIRECTIONS

In a large saucepan, heat to almost boiling chicken stock, white wine, parsley, bay leaf and thyme.

In a large everyday pan melt the butter on medium-high heat. Brown the chicken pieces about 4 minutes on each side. Lower the heat and cook about 10 minutes, turning as needed to prevent over-browning. Sprinkle with salt and pepper and the flour, ensuring the chicken pieces are all coated with liquid flour mixture.

Remove chicken from the pan. Scrape the browned bits from the sides and pour in the hot stock/wine liquid. Stir to blend and smooth. Return the chicken to the pan and simmer for 25-30 minutes.

In a small sauté pan cook mushrooms with butter, lemon juice and wine until tender—about 3-5 minutes at the most.

Remove chicken from the everyday pan and place on serving platter. Bring sauce to a boil, reduce heat to medium and allow sauce to reduce/cook down to about half. Thin with a touch of cream if desired and add the mushrooms. Serve with rice casserole and seasoned green peas.

COQ AU VIN (CHICKEN IN WINE)

Krista says: *I too wanted to have a really great "go to with confidence" menu I could produce for an elegant dinner party. I began experimenting with Mom's go-to chicken and other French chicken recipes and learned about cooking sauces. I became acquainted with Coq au Vin because of a restaurant in the first floor of one of the buildings I was leasing in Chicago. Due to the regional nature of French cooking, I have never been quite able to duplicate the Coq au Vin I first knew, but this one is delicious. When Scott wanted to host 10 of his teammates for a dinner party, he asked for this to be the main course and ever since it's been the main dish for my go-to menu. I joke around that I love it so much because the recipe uses an entire bottle of wine when it's all said and done. What's not to love about that?*

INGREDIENTS

5 tablespoons unsalted butter, divided:
-1 tablespoon
-2 tablespoons
-2 tablespoons, softened
1 tablespoon light olive oil
18+ pearl onions
8 ounces sliced mushrooms
4 tablespoons beef base

1 bottle of good Pinot Noir
-set aside ¼ cup
-3 cups will remain in the bottle
Salt and pepper to taste
¼ cup chopped fresh parsley

1 ½ bay leaves
1/2 teaspoon dried thyme
-divided in 2 (1/4 teaspoons)

4 oz. Applewood smoked bacon
3-4 pounds boneless chicken (can be a combination of breasts and thighs or all breasts, if you prefer, cut into bite-sized pieces)
¼ cup cognac

2 cups chicken or beef stock
3 tablespoons tomato paste
4 cloves crushed garlic

DIRECTIONS

In a large sauté pan melt 1 tablespoon butter in olive oil over medium heat. Sauté onions for 2-3 minutes. Add mushroom and cook until onions have softened. Add beef base, ¼ cup of wine, salt, pepper, parsley, ½ bay leaf and ¼ teaspoon of the thyme. Reduce heat to simmer and cover.

In a small mixing bowl, blend 2 tablespoons softened butter with flour until like a paste. Spoon some hot liquid into the bowl to blend, then pour into the sauté mixture and stir consistently for 1-2 minutes until sauce is thick and coats your spoon. Replace cover and remove from burner to a trivet or hot pad.

Melt last 2 tablespoons of butter in a large Dutch oven. Sauté bacon at low heat until slightly browned. Remove bacon and set aside to a paper towel-lined plate, leaving drippings and melted butter in the Dutch oven bottom. Add chicken, season with salt and pepper, and cook for 4-8 minutes, turning to brown evenly. Add back the bacon, cover and reduce heat to low. Cook another 5 minutes. Add cognac, light with a long match, and wait until the flame goes out.

Add remaining wine, whole bay leaf, last ¼ teaspoon thyme, stock, tomato paste, and garlic. Cover and simmer 25 to 30 minutes.

Using slotted spoon remove chicken and set aside.

Increase heat, bring liquid in Dutch oven to a boil. Boil until liquid is reduced to 2 cups. Reduce heat. Remove bay leaf. Add the onion-mushroom mixture and stir to incorporate smoothly. Return chicken to the mixture and ensure it's all coated with the wine, onion-mushroom sauce mixture. Simmer for 2-3 minutes more and you're ready to serve.

Serves 6-8 people comfortably with some leftovers.

Serve with your favorite Pinot Noir or Rhone style wine, mashed or twice-baked potatoes and green beans.

Welcome your guests to the table with the French Onion Tart to start, followed by the Simple Salad or The Salad.

TIPS, HINTS AND EXTRAS
Pearl onions can be found in the frozen section. Be sure to thaw and drain liquids ahead of cooking with them. I often use double the

amount of pearl onions when I use frozen, because the fresh pearls I purchase are much larger.

Two tablespoons dried parsley works if you don't have fresh.

Fresh parsley is nice for serving garnish, depending upon your presentation.

When it's time to light the cognac, use caution, especially if you have a low stove hood. You may want to move the Dutch oven to a trivet near open air before lighting the cognac.

The wine you select to cook with must be wine you would enjoy drinking, too. The quality and the personality of the wine is going to show up in the food. ☺ Learned that the hard way!

Bon Appétit.

BOEUF BOURGUIGNON (BEEF STEW IN RED WINE)

Mary says: This is an impressive dish, and we just get hungry for it. The recipe is from my cooking school experience in Cedar Falls. According to our teacher, Felicia Lavallee, this is "a peasant dish fit for any patrician palate." Patrician stew fit for the most patrician palate indeed!

INGREDIENTS

2 tablespoons unsalted butter (or olive oil)
2 pounds of lean stewing beef, cut in small cubes
1 tablespoon flour
Salt and pepper to taste
1 ½ cups dry red wine (French Burgundy or American Pinot Noir)
2 medium onions, sliced thin
4 stalks celery – ½ inch diced
6 carrots, bite-size pieces
2 tablespoons minced garlic – or two small cloves mashed
6 green onions, chopped
Bouquet garnish of parsley, ½ teaspoon thyme, bay leaf
¼ cup brandy or cognac (optional)

DIRECTIONS

Melt butter in heavy casserole or Dutch oven and in it brown the meat. Remove the meat and sprinkle flour over the fat in the casserole—mix well with a wooden spoon. Add salt and pepper and 1 cup of the wine. (It looks and smells awful at this point.)

Add sliced vegetables and spices. Add enough warm water so that liquid covers the meat and vegetables.

Cover the casserole tightly and bake at 250 for at least 2 ½ hours. After the first hour, uncover and stir in the other ½ cup of the wine.

After two hours, add brandy and bake for at least 30 minutes more.

Serve with rice or wide noodles and a baguette.

It serves at least 6 and any leftovers are terrific.

TIPS, HINTS AND EXTRAS
Use high quality red wine.

The original recipe said to strain the vegetables out of the sauce before serving. Felicia said it was more "genteel," but unnecessary—we like the vegetables in the stew!

Petite baby carrots also work well.

SESAME GINGER PORK PLATTER
Mary says: ENJOY! It's been a smash hit every time I've served it.

Krista says: A week before my neighbor (Scott Martens) in Chicago introduced me to my Scott, he and his wife, Adrienne, attended a party at my condo. I have a vivid memory of Mr. Martens standing stove-side eating bites of this tenderloin and licking his fingers at the end of the night. We Iowa people know how to enjoy our pork. LOL

INGREDIENTS

2 12 to 16 ounce pork tenderloins

Marinade:
½ cup soy sauce
¼ cup dark brown sugar
2 tablespoons canola oil
1 and ½ teaspoon crushed ginger or ½ teaspoon ground ginger
1 tablespoon sesame seeds

Platter Garnish:
Bunch of green and red grapes
Bibb or butter lettuce leaves
Green onion strips

Baguette or small cocktail buns

DIRECTIONS

Mix all the marinade Ingredients together and put tenderloins in a large Ziploc bag or glass dish with cover to marinate—at least 24 hours. Turn and stir them 2 – 3 times during the marinating period.

Remove the pork and save the marinade.

Bake until the pork registers 160 degrees on a meat thermometer.

Bring the marinade to a boil and let it thicken slightly. Use as a dipping sauce in a small container. The green onion strips serve as the brushes for the sauce.

Once done, cool barely and slice the tenderloins according to your serving plan, then display on a large platter garnished with lettuce leaves plus some red and green grape clusters.

Serve while warm.

TIPS, HINTS AND EXTRAS
This is a great marinade for thick pork chops as well, which you can grill.

You can add ½ cup of your favorite BBQ sauce to the marinade if you'd like to add a little extra splash or zip.

"THIS IS IT!" MEAT LOAF

Mary says: *This is the famous "This is it!" Meat Loaf. The McElhinney sisters all had multiple meat loaf recipes and were challenged to find the best one. They made a lot of recipes, then combined the parts they liked best about all of them and came up with this **one** recipe.*

INGREDIENTS

1 pound ground beef
½ pound ground pork
½ pound ground veal
1 tablespoon Worcestershire sauce
¾ cup tomato juice
½ cup dry breadcrumbs or saltine crackers crushed to make ½ cup
2 eggs, beaten
¾ cup finely chopped onions
1 ½ teaspoon dry mustard
1 teaspoon salt
½ teaspoon black pepper
6 strips of bacon
1 8-ounce can tomato sauce

DIRECTIONS

Preheat oven to 350°.

Using your hands, dive into a big mixing bowl and mix meats, eggs, onions, w-shire sauce, dry mustard, salt and pepper, bread crumbs, plus tomato juice together. You'll pretty much knead this all together into a big blob.

Mold into loaves, either sized to existing loaf pans or small casserole dishes. Cover on top with bacon strips. Pour tomato sauce over the loaf.

Bake at least 1 hour and 15 minutes.

TIPS, HINTS AND EXTRAS
Mary uses this meat loaf to stuff peppers as well as simply baking small meat loaves.

Mary says: I don't pour the tomato sauce over the loaves prior to baking, and I don't use the bacon strips. It's too runny for me. Instead, I make a dent in the middle with the handle of a wooden spoon and fill it with Cookie's BBQ sauce.

Krista says: I use the bacon, partially pre-cooked, woven/layered to create a neater-looking top to the loaf. And, instead of tomato sauce I use Ketchapeno (a thick ketchup made with jalapeño peppers).

Side Plates

TWICE-BAKED POTATOES

Krista says: *What's not to love about a twice-baked potato? I recall watching my Grandma Geneva make these and then carefully arrange them on a special oval china platter ahead of placing them on the buffet, and I thought she was so fancy. What I also enjoyed was there was leftover potato filling, so there might be a sample or spoon to lick.*

Over the years I've watched Mom make these too, and Twice-Baked Potatoes are just the right accompaniment for a big dinner of comfort food prepared for a crowd. These days our family dinner crowd keeps growing, so an elegant yet simple side like this is an excellent choice. Here we list some optional Ingredients you can include depending upon the tastes of your crowd.

INGREDIENTS

8 large unpeeled baking potatoes (6 to 8 ounces each) gently scrubbed.
Canola oil
1/4 to 1/2 cup milk or half & half
3-4 tablespoons unsalted butter
Dash white pepper
Salt to taste
Dried parsley for garnish

Optional additions:
3 tablespoons chopped fresh chives, or
3 tablespoons chopped fresh green onion tops,
3 tablespoons cooked crispy bacon pieces
1/4 cup sour cream or Crème fraîche
1 cup finely shredded Cheddar cheese

DIRECTIONS

Heat oven to 375°, set rack in center of oven, poke potatoes in a few spots with a fork for venting, rub a small amount of oil all over potatoes. Bake directly on oven rack for 45 minutes to an hour, until tender when a fork is inserted.

Let cool about 7-10 minutes. Using a clean kitchen towel or oven mitt, hold potato and cut lengthwise in half; scoop out insides into a medium to large bowl. Leave thinly outlined fleshy shell of each of the 16 potato halves.

Mash potatoes with potato masher or hand mixer on low speed until smooth. Add milk in small amounts and blend to desired fluffiness. Different types of potatoes need more milk to fluff.

Add butter, salt and pepper and beat thoroughly until mixture is light and fluffy. (If you are adding any of the options to be baked in, now is the time to gently stir them in, not beat them in.) The combination of bacon, chives and sour cream is yummy! You can also use the Options as garnish choices for your guests.

Line a cookie sheet with foil or parchment paper. Use a tablespoon to fill the 16 potato shells with the mashed mixture. Place on lined cookie sheet.*

Return to 375° oven and bake about 20 minutes when the filling will be heated thoroughly and the tops are beginning to brown.

Let cool slightly and arrange on your special platter. Top with a small dollop of butter and as it starts to melt sprinkle with parsley.

TIPS, HINTS AND EXTRAS

*As a time savings the day of your dinner party, make these the day before, cover and refrigerate, then complete the final 20 minutes baking prior to serving.

For extra fancy, place half your mashed mixture into a pastry bag and use a large star or wide patterned tip to pipe the filling into the potatoes. You can also get creative with fork patterns atop the potatoes.

SPEEDY SCALLOPED POTATOES
Krista says: *Here's another family favorite over the years. Guaranteed comfort food. When I was a little girl, depending upon the hostess, the variety of colored casserole dishes used to present the scalloped potatoes was fun for me. Remember avocado green and extra golden, even burnt orange casseroles? And of course the ever practical clear Pyrex or white Corningware with the blue flower on the sides? This is one of those recipes that simply following the basic, straightforward directions ensures you will create a fabulous feast of potatoes.*

INGREDIENTS

8 medium potatoes, pared and thinly sliced
¼ cup chopped green pepper
¼ cup chopped yellow onion
1 can mushroom soup
1 cup milk
1-2 teaspoons salt (to taste)
½ teaspoon black pepper (to taste)

DIRECTIONS

Butter (or use cooking spray) an 11 x 7 x 1 ½" baking dish or 2 quart casserole.

Preheat oven to 350°.

Alternate layers of potatoes, green peppers and onions.

Combine soup, milk, and seasonings in a small bowl or large measuring cup with a handle. Pour over potatoes.

Cover with foil and bake for 45 minutes. Uncover and bake 20 minutes more.

Serves 8 easily.

TIPS, HINTS AND EXTRAS

Here's another dish where optional additions are easy and fun to experiment with. Try adding 4 cloves of smashed garlic as an extra or in place of the pepper. Try adding paprika sprinkled on top for a little extra pizzazz.

You can also sprinkle with a 50/50 mixture ¼ cup breadcrumbs and ¼ cup grated Parmesan mixture after the first 45 minutes of baking and create a Gratin-style dish.

Mixing in 1 cup of shredded Swiss or Gruyere cheese makes this dish even richer.

The options are numerous. Enjoy!

MEYER LEMON PARMESAN RISOTTO

Krista says: *Right alongside the comfort foods you've read about comes an elegant Italian rice presentation. Don't hesitate to try this. Take your time; enjoy the process. Make this when you have company sipping wine with you in your kitchen so you don't miss out on conversation. This is another dish you can "play" with or experiment with. Once you master the basic beginning preparation, the "finishing" and dressing up your risotto is fun. Although we share it here as a side dish, you could make risotto the main course of any meal. With our affinity for the Meyer Lemon, this is popular in our kitchen.*

INGREDIENTS

6 cups low sodium chicken broth
3 ½ tablespoons unsalted butter
1 ½ tablespoons olive oil
2 large shallots, finely chopped
2 cups Arborio rice
¼ cup dry white wine
1 cup grated Parmesan cheese (3 ounces +/-)
2 tablespoons chopped parsley (dried will work, use 3 tablespoons)
4 tablespoons fresh Meyer lemon juice
4 heaping teaspoons grated lemon peel (go on, use 6 teaspoons)

DIRECTIONS

Simmer the broth in a large saucepan over medium-low heat and cover. Have a 1-cup ladle ready.

Melt 1 ½ tablespoons butter and oil in a large everyday pan over medium heat. Add shallots and sauté until tender, about 5-7 minutes.

Add rice and stir thoroughly. Add wine and stir thoroughly until the liquid has cooked off (less than a minute). Add 2 ladles of broth, stirring until liquid disappears/absorbs. Add remaining broth 1 ladle at a time until rice is creamy and al dente. (Al dente is Italian for firm to the bite. Certainly not mushy like mashed potato texture.)

This process may take up to 40 minutes or more—thus the suggestion to have company to sip wine with whilst you stir. Reduce heat to low and stir in cheese and balance of the butter.

Finish by adding the parsley, lemon juice and lemon peel. Season with fresh cracked pepper. (It may not need salt, depending upon the broth you selected.)

Transfer to a pretty serving bowl and serve. Buon appetito!

TIPS, HINTS AND EXTRAS
Here is where you can have fun with risotto. In the above recipe when I wrote "finish by adding," insert some other Ingredients in place of the lemon if you'd like.

Ideas:
-2 ounces thinly sliced prosciutto and 1 cup of frozen baby peas
-1 cup chopped on the angle fresh asparagus
-1 ½ ounces reconstituted dried porcini mushrooms
-1 pound of sweet Italian sausage (replace the wine in the recipe with Madeira)

As with our scalloped potatoes, the options are numerous and it's fun to vary the "finish" and get creative.

STEAMED FRENCH GREEN BEANS 3 WAYS

Krista says: A memory I savor about my Grandma Wilma is snipping green beans with her in the big white kitchen sink. Fresh green beans were grown on Aunt Esther and Uncle Frank's farm, or we'd pick them up at roadside farmers' stands in the country. We had the opportunity to grow them, pick them, wash them and then snip the ends ahead of cooking. And fresh green beans are delicious, even with just a hint of melted butter, salt and pepper. Here's three of my favorite ways to "finish" green beans after steaming.

INGREDIENTS

1 pound fresh green beans, washed and snipped, steamed in double boiler for 5-10 minutes until cooked but still firm

Maitre d'Hotel style:
2-3 teaspoons lemon juice
3-4 tablespoons softened butter cut into 3 pieces
2-3 tablespoons minced parsley (fresh or dried will do)

Almondine:
¼ cup sliced almonds
1-2 tablespoons olive oil
Balsamic Vinegar to taste

Onions and Bacon:
4 slices Applewood smoked bacon
1 (16 ounce) bottle cocktail onions, drained
2 teaspoons sugar or honey

¼ teaspoon dried thyme leaves
1 ½ tablespoon white balsamic vinegar
¾ teaspoon salt (a couple cranks on your sea salt grinder)
Dash to ¼ teaspoon white pepper (to taste, black pepper OK, too)

DIRECTIONS

For Maitre d'Hotel style: Place steamed beans into serving dish. Gradually toss with each piece of softened butter alternating with additions of lemon juice. Add salt and pepper to taste. Sprinkle with parsley prior to serving.

For Almondine: In medium-sized sauté pan, heat oil over med-high heat, add almonds and stir constantly until they begin to toast/brown. Remove from heat. Drizzle with small dashes of balsamic vinegar to taste. Toss with steamed beans in a serving dish.

For Onions and Bacon: In large sauté pan cook the bacon over medium-high heat until crisp. Reduce heat to low. Remove the bacon, and leave about 2 tablespoons drippings. Drain any remaining grease. Place bacon on paper towels to tamp remaining grease. Remember to drain the cocktail onions and add them to sauté pan with drippings; cook and stir for 2-3 minutes. Add honey and stir gently, then add thyme, cook and stir for another 3 minutes or until onions begin to brown. Add the beans; heat for 2-3 minutes. Add vinegar, salt, and pepper; using tongs toss to coat the beans with the sauce. Toss in crumbled bacon just before serving.

KIMBERLY'S SWEET POTATO SOUFFLÉ
Mary says: Kent and Kim lived in Raleigh, NC for several years and Kim enjoyed some of the "southern" specialties available there. This one has become a necessity for Thanksgiving dinners.

INGREDIENTS

Casserole:
3 cups baked and mashed sweet potatoes (4-5 medium sized sweet potatoes)
½ cup sugar
½ stick unsalted butter
½ cup milk
½ teaspoon salt
2 eggs, beaten

Topping:
½ cup flour
1 cup dark brown sugar
½ stick butter softened and cut into small pieces
1 cup chopped pecans

DIRECTIONS

Preheat oven to 350°. Butter a 13' x 9' baking dish or equivalent casserole or baking dish.

For the casserole, in a medium-sized mixing bowl combine the mashed sweet potatoes, sugar, butter, milk, salt and beaten eggs. Pour evenly into baking dish.

For the topping, in a smaller mixing bowl, first combine flour and brown sugar, and then add softened butter plus pecans to create a crumbly topping.

Cover casserole mix evenly with the crumbly topping and bake uncovered for 35 to 45 minutes, or until topping is beginning to brown slightly.

Makes 10 generous servings.

TIPS, HINTS AND EXTRAS

This dish is fun to prepare in individual ramekins. When you're serving buffet style, this makes your buffet look more interesting (compared to a view of 4-5 casserole dishes). Here's a way to be innovative with the presentation of a traditional favorite for Thanksgiving, Christmas, Holiday time and Easter menus for large groups. This recipe will easily fill 10-12 ramekins.

Desserts

AUNT ESTHER'S DEVIL'S FOOD CAKE

Mary says: Kay stayed with Aunt Esther in LeMars whenever the weather was too bad for him to drive back and forth to Remsen. She enjoyed having him and treated him royally. She would fix him whatever dinner he wanted at whatever time he showed up at her door.

This is a Kramer family staple food. I now bake it in a round quiche pan and serve it in pie-shaped wedges on plates painted with both caramel and chocolate syrup. Add a scoop of vanilla ice cream and drizzle chocolate syrup on top. Fit for a king! And one of Kay's all-time favorites.

Krista says: This is among the "go to" desserts at our house. There are so many fun variations with Aunt Esther's cake. Pan choices, layering, serving size & style. Baking in the round and serving on painted plates as Mom describes is by far my favorite for a dinner party. The house always smells so welcoming for company after you've baked it. And if you bake it just ahead of guests arriving, it's still slightly warm by the time you get to the dessert course.

INGREDIENTS

1 cup white sugar
4 tablespoons cocoa powder (mix in with the sugar)
½ cup unsalted butter softened
1 egg, beaten
1 cup cold water
1 teaspoon baking soda, dissolved in cold water
1 ¼ cups flour
1 teaspoon vanilla

DIRECTIONS

Cream the butter together with the sugar and cocoa. Add egg and beat well. Alternately add water and flour and beat well. Add vanilla. Bake in a buttered 9x9 cake pan for 20 minutes or until a toothpick placed in the center comes out clean.

TIPS, HINTS AND EXTRAS
In Krista's opinion, Hershey's Special Dark Cocoa is a winner product when making this cake!

GRANDMA WILMA'S PEAR PEACH CUSTARD PIE

Mary says: *We love this recipe so much we took it to Barbados and Chef Glen enjoyed adding to his repertoire. It is a HIT with everyone who tastes it. The story on this one is...I watched Grandma Wilma make this pie and created the recipe on paper. She never actually had a recipe for the pie before. Together, we decided this was the "correct" written version. I still have the stained recipe card in her handwriting.*

INGREDIENTS AND DIRECTIONS COMBINED

1 unbaked pie shell
Fill shell to heaping with peeled and sliced fresh peaches and pears (may only use peaches or pears or a combination of the two).
Sprinkle over the fruit about 1 tablespoon flour.
Beat 4 whole eggs with ¾ cup sugar and pour this mixture over the fruits and flour.
Sprinkle lightly with nutmeg.

Bake at 350° in the upper third of the oven for 50 to 60 minutes until custard is lightly browned.

It keeps well in the refrigerator but is at its best served slightly warm from the oven topped with vanilla ice cream. WOW!

THE BELL FILE CHOCOLATE PUDDING

Mary says: *Here is the ever-famous Bell chocolate pie filling recipe. I can make it from memory and it never fails me. I rarely put it in a pie crust anymore. Who needs the calories? Or the work?*

Krista says: *One of my favorite parts of this recipe is separating egg yolks from whites using Grandma Geneva's dark red Tupperware egg separator, which I have carefully stored and used with joy all these years.*

INGREDIENTS

1 cup sugar
3 tablespoons cornstarch
Dash of salt
2 cups milk
1 ½ squares baking chocolate
2 egg yolks
1 tablespoon butter
1 teaspoon vanilla

DIRECTIONS

Make a paste of the sugar, cornstarch and salt by adding a little cold water.

In the top of a double boiler, combine chocolate with the milk, stirring constantly. Add the sugar/starch mix with hot chocolate milk mixture stirring constantly until thick, about 15 minutes. Stir a little hot mixture into beaten egg yolks and return the yolks to the hot mixture, stirring constantly. Add vanilla and butter and let cool.

TIPS, HINTS AND EXTRAS

Mary says: Here's the good news: I have lightened this and made it in the microwave. Simple! Use a 4-cup Pyrex measuring cup. Use skim milk and reduce the sugar to ¾ cup. Melt the chocolate in the milk—usually takes about 3 to 4 minutes. Stir (I always use a whisk) about halfway through. In a two-cup measuring cup, make the paste of the sugar, cornstarch and salt. Pour it into the hot milk mixture and stir. Microwave for 2 to 3 minutes, and stir—then microwave 2 to 3 minutes more. Pour a little of the hot mixture into the egg yolks, then pour it all back into the big Pyrex and microwave another minute. Take it out and whisk well—add the vanilla and butter then let cool.

I usually serve this in small white ramekins. It also makes a great parfait, layered with whipped cream or ice cream in parfait glasses. OR make the pie!

HARTMAN LIMONCELLO CHEESECAKE

Krista says: *When I moved into my brand new construction condo in Chicago and was outfitting my new kitchen, I treated myself to a beautiful Kitchen Aid food processor. I decided to start experimenting with this little paperback cheesecake book Mom had given me. Among many of my girlfriends I developed a reputation for making "insane" cheesecakes. And I credit using the food processor for some of the richness I've developed in my cheesecake creations.*

One of my best friends, Laura, introduced me to Limoncello, an Italian digestivo or after dinner liqueur, originating in the Southern Italian regions around the Gulf of Naples, the Sorrentine Peninsula and the coast of Amalfi. She'd brought some back to the States after a trip to Sorrento. Over the years Laura and I have enjoyed discovering new brands, comparing which ones we thought were our favorites. We've both experimented in making our own homemade Limoncello. So she needs to be credited with getting me started on my love of Limoncello. After Scott and I started growing Meyer Lemons, we decided one year after a substantial harvest from our solo dwarf tree that we'd make Limoncello. We have been making Limoncello on an annual basis ever since.

One year in Dallas when Mom and Dad were visiting, we were at a restaurant where Limoncello Cheesecake was on the menu. This was an "aha" moment, as I'd never thought to make a cheesecake with Limoncello—until then. And so, after some experimentation, I'm proud of this Limoncello Cheesecake recipe. It has not, however, achieved the level of "This is it!" yet, because I am still experimenting. The best part of making this is to do so with our homegrown Meyer Lemons and homemade Limoncello.

INGREDIENTS

Crust:
½ cup gingersnap crumbs
½ cup graham cracker crumbs
3 tablespoons sugar
3 tablespoons butter, melted

Filling:
3 (8 ounce) blocks cream cheese, softened (sorry, but the lite stuff isn't acceptable)
1 cup sugar
2 tablespoons fine Meyer lemon zest
1 teaspoon vanilla
3 eggs, set out for room temperature ahead of preparation
1 egg white, room temperature (save the yolk for the topping)

Topping:
½ cup sugar
3 tablespoons cornstarch
½ cup water
4 tablespoons Limoncello
1 egg yolk, room temp

DIRECTIONS

For the crust: Preheat oven to 325°. In small food processor bowl with blade, mix crumbs with sugar and melted butter. Spread into a buttered 9 or 10-inch springform pan and bake for 10 minutes in the center of the oven. Remove to a cooling rack whilst you make the filling.

For the filling: Lower the oven temperature to 300°. In the large food processor bowl with blade, use the pulse control to mix the first four Ingredients together.

Use a good rubber spatula to scrape down the sides of the bowl to break up any cream cheese lumps. Pulse until nice and creamy.

Separately add each of the 3 eggs and the egg white in four different pulses. Scrape the sides with spatula one last time, then give the mix a final pulse.

Set the springform on a cookie sheet, pour the filling into the crust, and bake for about an hour until the center is beginning to set.

Turn off the oven, leave the door closed and let the cake rest as it cools for about an hour. Remove to a cooling rack. Run a knife (a wooden kabob skewer works well for non-stick pan) around the edge to loosen before removing springform pan side from the cake.

Place on your serving plate or foil-covered cake board and chill in the refrigerator until ahead of serving.

For the topping: In a small saucepan, mix sugar and cornstarch together. Add water and Limoncello gradually as you whisk Ingredients together over med-low heat and bring to a slow boil about 3-4 minutes. It will thicken quickly. Add a small amount of hot mix to the yolk, then add it all to the sauce pan mix. Whisk and continue to stir on low heat until a gel-like consistency. Remove from heat and let cool completely to room temperature.

Pour the topping over the cheesecake and enjoy serving. SO, SO GOOD, I PROMISE!

TIPS, HINTS AND EXTRAS
Use crumbs to absorb all the butter out of the container you melt it in, scrape into processor with a good rubber spatula.

When inserting rubber spatula into bowl of food processor, use caution not to catch or cut the spatula tip with the sharp metal blade.

A non-stick springform pan is a Godsend to a cheesecake baker, in my humble opinion. When using a non-stick pan, remember not to use anything metal, like knives or serving pieces, so you don't compromise the non-stick surface.

I highly recommend investing in high quality all-natural 100% pure vanilla. Makes a big difference in taste.

Why not serve with small pre-chilled cordial glasses containing about ½ ounce of Limoncello and toast your dinner guests and a lovely party?

ANNA'S ROLLED SUGAR COOKIES

Mary says: *This recipe comes from Anna Jorgenson, our lovely next-door neighbor in Cedar Falls circa 1964 to 1970. Anna and Jens had five sons, all veterinarians, and many grandchildren. Kent used to knock on her door and ask if she had "any grandchildren today?" If not, he would ask if she had any cookies. She always did.*

We have cut and decorated these cookies nearly every Christmas while Kent and Krista were growing up, and when the Kramer granddaughters were growing up as well. We even made these in the Barbados kitchen. They bring great memories of Mrs. Jorgenson, and many happy Christmas holidays.

Krista says: *I barely remember Mrs. Jorgenson, but I remember swinging down a short slope from her willow tree, and her cookies. I do recall making these cookies for most any occasion cookie cutters were manufactured for— Thanksgiving, Christmas, Valentine's Day, Saint Patrick's Day, Easter and other special times. One year in Urbandale during their Christmas visit, my cousin Jeff and his wife Kaye (with Mary's help) presented everyone with either a pink or light blue baby-foot-sized cutout cookie to announce they were expecting. The extended family spent that day celebrating together.*

INGREDIENTS

3 cups sifted flour
2 teaspoons baking powder
1 scant teaspoon baking soda
1 cup unsalted butter – soft at room temperature, cut into pieces

2 eggs, beaten
4 tablespoons milk
1+ teaspoon vanilla

DIRECTIONS

In a large mixing bowl, combine flour, baking powder and soda. Cut into this mixture the butter. It will form a pie-crust-like mixture. In a large measuring cup, combine eggs, sugar, milk, and vanilla. Add to the dough mixture; mix thoroughly and chill in the refrigerator about an hour.

Preheat oven to 350 °. Roll out on floured pastry cloth. With cookie cutters make desired shapes. Bake for 8-10 minutes. Cool on racks. Frost and decorate as you please.

Krista says: Making these cookies with my nieces has brought me great joy as well.

Over the years as I've become a certified kitchen gadget nerd, there have been more and more neat gadgets available for cookie-baking, and I admit to having purchased many of these, ranging from more cookie cutters than I know what to do with, to a rainbow of fancy sprinkle sugars and food colorings for decorating.

These cookies and the experiences I associate with them will always be special to me. Frosting and decorating is often the most fun. We "paint the cookies!"

EASY BUTTERCREAM FROSTING (COOKIE PAINT)

INGREDIENTS

1 1/2 cups powdered sugar
1/2 cup unsalted butter – soft at room temperature is key
1 teaspoon vanilla extract (be generous)
1-3+ teaspoons of whipping cream

DIRECTIONS

A good hand mixer or hand blender is perfect for making frosting. Blend the sugar and the butter together for about 3 minutes until thoroughly smooth. Add vanilla and 1 teaspoon of cream and beat thoroughly for about 1 minute. Use additional cream if it's too thick. Color with your choices of food coloring and "paint the cookies!"

About Mary, the Unlikely Ambassador

Before serving as an Iowa state senator, president of the Iowa State Senate, and US ambassador to Barbados and the Eastern Caribbean, Ambassador Mary Kramer (Ret.) was a nightclub piano player, music teacher, public school administrator, retail personnel director, and vice president of human resources and community relations in the insurance industry. Inducted into the Iowa Women's Hall of Fame in 2009, her first memoir, *More Than a Walk on the Beach*, was published in 2010. Married to her best friend for nearly sixty years, Kramer is a mother of two and grandmother of four.

About Krista, the Diplomatic Daughter

The ambassador's daughter, Krista Kramer Hartman, began her career as a semi-pro golfer and played a little lounge piano herself. From a successful career in real estate she's emerged as a serial entrepreneur honored numerous times for her professional acumen and community leadership. She enjoys every opportunity to empower and develop others and currently works as a business consultant and coach. Next, she plans to become a winemaker and plant a vineyard and with her husband.